Finding Encouragement in the
Ultimate Helping Profession

Motherhood STRESS

Finding Encouragement in the
Ultimate Helping Profession

Motherhood STRESS

Deborah Shaw Lewis

with Gregg Lewis

WORD PUBLISHING
Dallas · London · Sydney · Singapore

Library of Congress Cataloging-in-Publication Data

Lewis, Deborah Shaw, 1951–
    Motherhood stress : finding encouragement in the ultimate helping
profession / Deborah Shaw Lewis and Gregg A. Lewis.
        p. cm.
    ISBN 0-8499-0671-7
    1. Motherhood. 2. Stress (Psychology) I. Lewis, Gregg A.
II. Title.
HQ759.L486   1989
306.874'3—dc20   89-32403
                                                           CIP

Printed in the United States of America

9 8 0 1 2 3 9 BKC 9 8 7 6 5 4 3 2

To my mother,
RUTH BAIRD SHAW,
who took such joy in her mothering.

And to the children who made me a mother
and cause me great stress and much greater joy—
ANDREW, MATTHEW, LISETTE, BENJAMIN and JONATHAN

Acknowledgments

Thank you to the many mothers willing to talk with me about their lives and their stresses.

Thank you to the women of The Circle of Friends, my church circle, who have given me the support and friendship I have needed to relieve my motherhood stress.

Thank you to Judy Smith, my one-on-one motherhood stress reliever, phone partner and child-swapper, who shared my joys and frustrations in the earliest years of my mothering.

Thank you to my sisters and sisters-in-law who have always been there for me—if only at the end of a long distance phone line: Janice Crouse, Joan Turrentine, Sheila Shaw, Carol Johnston, Beth Shaw, Vicki Shaw and Angela Lewis.

Thank you to my friends: Debbie VanDerMolen, Linda Eberhardt, Regina Threlkeld, Linda Simpson, Martha Ivey, Ruth Senter, Karen Tucker, Jan Karlsen, Cathy Bruce, Marlene Hardesty, and Lee Ann Lueck—for sharing their lives and their stories with me.

And thank you most of all to Gregg, my editor, my husband, my best friend and my best support.

Contents

Contents

Finding Encouragement in the
Ultimate Helping Profession

Motherhood
STRESS

1

I'm Just a Mother

In a rare moment of calm, my friend, Barb, and I sat at her kitchen table sipping warm tea and talking. Our young children—her three, and three of my five—had quickly paired off and were playing happily in her back yard.

"I've been worried lately," Barb admitted. "My hair has been coming out by the handful whenever I brush it. So I went to the doctor this week to find out what was wrong."

"Oh? What did he say?"

Barb shook her head. "He told me it was only stress. But I can't see how it could be. I'm just a mother. It's not like I work."

Only stress? Just a mother? Mothers don't work? I knew right then Barb and I needed to have a long talk. And I remembered the time, a few years ago, when I began to understand some of the stress I've felt as a mother.

* * *

I'd awakened one morning, wondering where the night had gone and trying to remember how many times I'd been up. The first time was when our oldest son Andrew (who was then two) had wandered into our room in the dark and climbed into bed with us. I'd been up twice with seven-month-old Matthew who'd begun teething. The second time, I'd just brought him to bed and nursed him there. Then I'd been up myself with a nightmare—

one in which I'd lost Andrew in a hospital and had run up and down endless, winding corridors frantically searching for him.

It didn't take Freud to figure that one out, I thought. Our pediatrician had been concerned about the large soft spot on Andrew's head. He'd sent us to a neurologist who had examined Andrew, run down a long list of serious problems that might explain why Andrew's fontanel wasn't closing, and scheduled a CAT-scan at a big Chicago hospital. We'd recently gotten the results: no problem, the fontanel would eventually close. Even though it had ended with good news, the entire experience—especially the CAT-scan—had been frightening for us all.

I need to get up and going, I chided myself. *It's Monday again*. Each week I vowed I'd get all my papers graded over the weekend. But most Mondays dawned, like this one, with half my papers left to grade and my Monday evening's class lecture yet to finalize. *I was crazy to think I could teach two college courses this term*, I thought. *Why do I feel overwhelmed teaching just five semester hours a week?*

After a late breakfast, I sat in an easy chair with my two boys on my lap. They watched "Sesame Street" and "Mr. Rogers' Neighborhood" while I dozed off, trying to get enough sleep to last me until I got home from work at 10:30 that night. In the afternoon, while my children napped, I graded the remaining papers and went over my lecture.

The course I was teaching that evening was called "Principles and Practices of Child Care." Most of my students were studying to work in day care centers, and few of them had a realistic picture of how stressful working with small children could be. So I'd been preparing a new lecture based on a professional journal article entitled "'Playing with Kids All Day': Job Stress in Early Childhood Education."

In my lecture notes I'd jotted down a list of job stresses mentioned in the article which I intended to discuss in class:

- an excess of novelty and uncertainty
- lack of control

- high expectations
- ideals versus reality
- no clear guidelines or measures for success
- frustrations
- low status and low pay
- poor accountability

Reading down the list, it hit me. This list of job stresses in early childhood education might have been my own job description as a mother.

You want novelty and uncertainty? Be a mother and try to figure out when you'll be able to get a good night's sleep or when you can count on finishing any project you start.

Lack of control? Sit in a hospital emergency room after they wheel your child away on a gurney and wait for some doctor you've never seen before to come and tell you whether or not your child's life hangs in the balance. Everything feels beyond your control!

No clear guidelines? Try sorting out all the conflicting child-rearing advice given to mothers by doctors, friends, relatives, how-to books, and all those "experts" who show up on TV talk shows.

Frustration? *Tell me about it,* I thought. Just the week before it had taken me over an hour to get ready to go to the grocery store. We had to search the entire house to find Andrew's shoes. No sooner had we climbed in the car than he had to go to the bathroom again. So it was back inside for that. Then out to the car again. As I buckled Matthew into his carseat, my nose told me he was messy. So we went inside once more to change his diaper. Then the phone rang. I talked to a friend briefly and felt as if I'd cut her off short. Again out to the car. I'd buckled both children up again and began backing out the driveway only to glance at the dashboard clock and realize it was nearly noon. I knew better than to attempt a long shopping trip with two hungry children. So I got the kids out of the car and headed back inside where I hung up our coats, sat down, and cried.

Accountability? Some days I feel as if no one notices—or cares about—what I'm doing with my children. Other days I feel as if everyone has a different standard I'm not living up to.

Ideals versus reality? Before my first baby was born, I thought often about becoming a mother and "taking some time off" to be at home. I never thought it would be a vacation—like relaxing on the beach in the Bahamas for a few years; but I hadn't really thought about it as "work" either.

I had dreamed of outings to the park and visits to the library and wonderful winter afternoons in a warm kitchen baking cookies with my children. And the house in the background of all my dreams was always spotlessly clean.

My reality includes parks and library trips and baking and lots of other wonderful things: cuddling children in my lap, reading stories, playing games, watching children grow, taking pride in their achievements. In all my wildest fantasies of motherhood, I could never have imagined all the joys of my reality; nothing prepared me for the rush of tender feeling I'd get when my nursing baby looked up into my eyes and grinned his first toothless grin.

But my reality includes a lot of other things which *weren't* a part of my dreams. I never realized how much time I'd spend changing diapers, washing clothes and more clothes, wiping up spills, picking up toys, driving children everywhere, pinching pennies between paychecks. I never imagined yelling at my kids in frustration. I'd never pictured myself walking out the door to take my children to a park and feeling guilty about the messy house I was leaving behind.

Yes, I felt the tension between the ideals and the reality. And as a mother I'd felt all those other stresses I'd noted in my lecture as well.

I taught my class that night and was pleased at the lively discussion which resulted—especially among those students in my class who were already teachers. They acted excited and relieved to hear someone say they had good reasons to feel stressed working with young children. And I drove home after class also feeling relieved in my new understanding, that I, too, had legitimate reasons for the stress I felt in my job as a mother.

*   *   *

In the weeks and months that followed that revelation, I read many newspaper and magazine articles on the general topic of job stress. And I quickly realized that virtually all the "job stresses" I read about—whatever the job—could apply to my job of motherhood.

Yet no one had ever told me about motherhood stress. And as I talked to other mothers about their experiences, I quickly learned no one had told them either.

Many stay-at-home mothers admitted to a wide variety of stress symptoms. But as my friend Barb had done, they told themselves, *I shouldn't feel stressed. I'm just a mother. It's not like I work.*

And the mothers I talked to who worked outside their homes seemed to feel that it was "okay" to feel stressed about their outside jobs or about trying to juggle both parts of their lives. But they did not recognize the stresses in the mothering part of their jobs. It was as if the mothering wasn't work, therefore it shouldn't be stressful.

I've worked outside my home *and* been a stay-at-home mother as well. I've talked to other mothers in both situations. I've learned each group experiences some stresses the other doesn't. But most motherhood stress is common to all mothers; it comes with the territory.

What mother can't identify with one or more of the various stresses described by the following women? (Names have been changed, as have been most names throughout this book.)

Carol told me: "I felt like a giant rubber band with my five-year-old on one end and my new baby on the other. I'd gotten used to dropping everything and doing what I needed to do for Sarah. But now here was little Anna, a whole other person who was pulling me in a whole different direction."

"Letting go is so stressful," said Andrea, the mother of two teenagers. "I want so badly for my children to make the right choices, because every choice they make now counts. And I have less and less influence over those choices."

Melissa, the mother of two preschool boys, said, "I get up in the morning with this list of things I'm going to do. And by the end of the day, I haven't done any of them. At first that was hard for me. As an accountant, I always want everything to be just so. I like having everything all in a row and balanced—debits equals credits. I wanted to have my child and not have my life change in any way. Just to be able to go on and do this and this and this. I learned real quickly, motherhood doesn't work that way!"

And then there was the mother who left her job as a correspondent in the Paris bureau of *Women's Wear Daily* to care for her baby. In the March 1989 issue of *American Health* she wrote, "Insecure in my new role, I was at odds with—and battered by—an ideal of the breezy, capable mother I assumed everyone else was. I could handle myself at important meetings, meet tough deadlines, argue fluently in French. Why couldn't I keep Cheerios off the kitchen floor?"

"It always seemed so easy for my mother," admitted Anna, mother of five- and one-year-old daughters. "Adult life in general and motherhood in particular have proven so much more difficult than I ever expected."

Joanne summed up motherhood this way: "Some days it seems as if everyone's happiness depends on me. When you're a mother it's always give, give, give. And even though you want to do it, giving is stressful."

I've talked with rich mothers and poor mothers, brand new mothers and grandmothers, mothers of one and mothers of nine, stay-at-home mothers and mothers with two careers, single mothers raising their children all alone and happily married women with wonderfully supportive husbands. Whatever a mother's circumstances, the mere mention of the two words "motherhood" and "stress" invariably brought an outpouring of feelings and stories. When it comes to motherhood stress, all mothers feel it.

We ought to be talking about it. We ought to understand it better.

So that's what we're going to do in this book. I'll be sharing from my own experience and those of the many women I've talked to about motherhood stress.

We'll begin in the next several chapters by examining many recognized job stress factors and seeing how they apply to motherhood. We'll discover new motherhood stresses created by our modern-day culture. We'll talk some about the effects of stress. Then we'll spend the last few chapters revealing some of the strategies women have shared with me—strategies for coping with motherhood stress. (After the end of the book there's even an afterword chapter written especially for mothers to share with their husbands to help sensitize men to the reality of motherhood stress.)

Mothering certainly has its wonderful times. But it's more than "playing with kids all day." It's hard work. Important work. Stressful work.

It's time we understood motherhood stress.

Part I

MOTHERHOOD STRESS:
Exploring Causes and Effects

2

Stress? What Stress?

One morning recently, I rolled out of bed and, like most mornings, hit the floor running. Enroute to the kitchen to begin heating water for oatmeal, I flicked on the lights in all the bedrooms. Then I returned to the kids' rooms to see who was upright and who remained comatose. One child was both.

The following few minutes felt like the typical morning routine. Except you can't really call it a "routine" when there's no real pattern that repeats itself even two days in a row—unless you count the familiar feelings of frenzy which quickly filled the house.

Andrew and Matthew, my nine- and seven-year-olds, were doing fine. I gave a quick glance of approval at the clothes they were pulling on. Nothing clashed. Everything clean. No problems.

My three-year-old, Benjamin, needed help with the zipper on his sleeper and, a couple of minutes later, a tug of assistance to get his jogging suit shirt over his head.

I spent several minutes consoling Lisette, my kindergartner, because the teddy bear sweater she wanted to wear was in the dirty clothes. Then I spent another few minutes coaxing her into making a second choice, during which time I also changed the baby's diaper, dressed him for the day, suddenly remembered to stir the dried oats into the boiling water, and tied Benjamin's shoes.

With all children finally dressed and seated at the table, I nursed the baby as I simultaneously ate my own breakfast and ran through the regular preschool checklist: Everyone got their book bags ready? Yes. Andrew's homework in? Yes. Lunch money in order? Yes. Field trip permission slip signed? No. Where is it? No one knows. Began search. Found it on the counter under the phone book. Signed it. Gulped another three bites of breakfast and then hurriedly donned a jogging suit of my own while everyone else brushed teeth.

The kitchen clock said 8:08 as I ushered four children out the door and followed with baby Jonathan in my arms. We were actually two minutes ahead of schedule for the drive to school—until we stopped for the work crew doing a little road maintenance. The usual ten-minute drive took thirteen, meaning I dropped three distressed children off outside their school to the ringing judgment of the tardy bell.

I took a deep breath to try to relax—knowing full well the race had just begun. This was my morning to do errands, and my to-do list was long: Mail bills and buy stamps at post office, get gas and a ten-minute oil change, return books to library, buy groceries, and then stop at K-Mart for diapers and a handful of other stock-up items on special sale this week. All that by 2:00 P.M. when I had to be back at school to pick up Lisette.

As I drove to Kroger, I wondered, *How do other mothers actually get make-up applied and their hair curled before dropping their kids at school?* With a grimace, I remembered the days B.C. (before children) when I vowed never to be one of those women who "let themselves go" after they had kids. Now, most mornings, I felt lucky just to have brushed my teeth and be wearing matching tennis shoes when I dashed out my front door.

By one o'clock, I had all but one errand completed. A miracle morning. I'd even encountered a post office clerk nice enough to qualify for the "civil" part of "civil servant." But as I sat in my car, nursing Jonathan and eating a lunch of drive-through burgers with Benjamin, I studied my watch and tried to calculate my time.

One hour. Well, 55 minutes. Could I do it? *Let's see. Ten minutes for Jonathan to finish nursing. Ten minutes from K-Mart to* school. *That leaves me 35 minutes in the store. I'll be cutting it close. But I can do it!*

And we did. At 1:40, with my cart filled around Jonathan's infant seat and Benjamin cheerfully trotting along behind, I headed for the checkout counters. The miracle continued; they were virtually empty. *Wonderful. I am really going to make it.* I took a long, deep breath to slow my still-racing heart.

That was the precise moment my three-year-old announced, "Mama, I have to go to the bathroom!" I wanted to cry. Why hadn't I realized he would need to go? He hadn't been since we were in the grocery store earlier.

"Can you wait till we get to Lisette's school?" I asked.

I was trying to decide whether to believe his matter-of-fact "No," when this sudden look of desperation crossed his face. We headed for the back of the store at full speed.

Calm down, Debi, I instructed myself as I waited, heart pounding again, in the bathroom. *You can still make it.*

I can't explain it; maybe our mad dash to the bathroom had sparked a panic. By the time we got to the front of the store a second time, the checkout lines were backed up from here to Christmas.

I chose the shortest line. Of course that meant I got the world's slowest living clerk. (I think it's an unwritten rule of the universe, one of those Murphy's Laws, or something.) As I watched her work, I also kept looking at my watch. *Why did I ever think I could make it? If I'd just driven to the school, Benjamin and I could have enjoyed reading books together while we waited.* Now, thirteen minutes before I was supposed to pick up Lisette, the clerk finished bagging the merchandise of the elderly woman in front of me.

Decision time. At least ten minutes to ring up my purchases and get my check approved. Another five minutes to get everything to the car, ten to get to school. I'd be twelve minutes late. *I can't do it. Lisette was upset at being tardy this morning. I don't want to be late again.*

I sighed, told the clerk I was past due to pick up my daughter, pushed my cart off to one side, and hurried out of the store. We hit all the lights wrong and arrived at school four minutes late anyway. After apologizing to Lisette, we all drove back across town to K-Mart, found my cart, waited to check out a second time and, at long last, headed home. By the time I finally got Benjamin and Jonathan down for late naps, I felt too keyed up to really listen to what Lisette wanted to tell me about school that day.

* * *

Just recounting that day makes me feel frazzled. But the fact is, my experience wasn't that unusual. I've had many other days like it. Most mothers have.

So I tell this story, not because it's unique, but because its very ordinariness clearly illustrates the parallels between motherhood stress and several of the biggest stresses in any other occupation.

Unpredictability

A certain amount of novelty can be a plus on any job. It cuts down on boredom and often stimulates creativity and productivity. But an excess of novelty can create tremendous stress.

We have a good friend named Harold who served a few years ago as campaign manager for a candidate running for a seat in the U.S. House of Representatives. Harold dragged home late one evening from campaign headquarters, feeling exhausted.

"What a stressful job!" he exclaimed. "And the worst part isn't the long hours or the emotional drain. It's the unpredictability of politics. I started today with a to-do list as long as my arm. Then we got a mid-morning phone call cancelling one of our scheduled events, and the rest of the day was up for grabs as I faced a whole new set of priorities. I never know at the beginning of the day how much I'll be able to get done or what crisis is going to disrupt my plans. It's just so unpredictable!"

Harold's wife, Judy, the mother of two active preschool boys, nodded sympathetically and smiled. "I know," she told him. "Every day is like that for me."

Her far-more-sensitive-than-average husband looked up in

surprise and sheepishly admitted, "I've never thought about it like that before."

Many mothers haven't stopped to recognize the stress that results from the unpredictability they live with every day. But it's there. Unpredictability is a big part of the job description.

Could there be any job *more* unpredictable?

Cindy gives this example: "I was already showered and dressed for work with a head start on my morning when I went to waken my first-grader to get ready for school. The moment he sat up and pulled off his pajama top, I saw the red spots—chicken pox. I had to cancel all the day's appointments and juggle my office schedule for the next week—at one of the busiest times of the year for my business."

I remember the morning I stepped out of the kitchen for a minute, and Benjamin, who was not quite two at the time, pushed a chair over to the counter, climbed up, grabbed a sharp knife I'd carefully left out of his reach, and attempted to cut his own apple. He sliced his finger instead. And I spent the first half of my day sitting in an emergency room waiting for stitches, feeling extremely stressed (and guilty).

Such unpredictability is by no means limited to mothers of toddlers and grade-schoolers either. While a mother may not be confined to the house while her teenage son is bedridden with a bad case of mono, it's not as if there aren't unplanned implications.

And as Beth, another mother, said, "You want to talk about stress. How's this for instant stress? I take a day off from work, my first sick day in over a year. I'm sitting wrapped in a blanket drinking hot tea when the phone rings. It's my son, a high school senior I'd let drive my car to school that morning. 'Hi, mom. Feeling better?' Something's wrong. A mother can tell in a second. 'What's wrong, honey?'

"An awkward pause. 'You think you could come get me?'

"'But you've got the car.'

"'I know. I had a little accident. I'm down at the police station.'

"Like I said, 'Instant stress.' Fortunately, he wasn't hurt. The car wasn't seriously damaged. And bail for his 'failure-to-yield-right-of-way' ticket was only fifty dollars. But all plans for my day of rest and recuperation went out the window."

Illness and accidents aren't the only unpredictables in a mother's job either. By their very nature, children may well be the most unpredictable creatures on God's green earth.

Any mother who's had more than one child will tell you: it's impossible to predict what one will do based on your experience with another. Each baby, each child, and certainly each adolescent is his or her own unpredictable individual.

Any pediatrician worth his stethoscope could tell you that parents invariably underestimate what a child can, or will try, to do. I remember walking into the living room and finding my seventeen-month-old, Matthew, playing happily on top of an upright piano before I'd ever known he'd become such an accomplished mini-mountaineer. And not one of my other children, before or since, ever duplicated that stunt.

You can't even predict with certainty the rate of your child's physical, emotional or social development. You can only guess within months when a baby will start walking. Age at puberty can vary by years. And who can foretell at what age (if ever) boy will meet girl and the two of them will come to you and announce, "We want to get married"?

And you can't predict a child's behavior or his whims any better than you can his rate of physical or social development, as shown by two quick examples from my own recent experience:

First, behavior. I often let my five- and three-year-olds play together in the tub before we get down to the more serious business of washing and shampooing. They're old enough to call if they need something, so I don't hesitate to leave the bathroom to start a load of laundry or even skim the front page of the newspaper while they play. They're always fine. Or rather they were until the other evening, when they decided to amuse themselves by filling the bucket we store tub toys in with water, and dumping it over each other's heads. What I didn't realize was that, while they were having a grand time laughing and playing, splashing water had covered the bathroom floor, seeped under the baseboards and was dripping into their father's basement office. Talk about totally unpredictable behavior!

And then the whims. Another night last week we fixed hot chocolate for a bedtime treat. I only found three identical cups for four kids. The fourth cup was yellow, Benjamin's favorite color. I decided he'd be glad for the yellow one. Ninety-nine times out of a hundred, that would be true. But not that night. And instead of the calm, happy family bedtime I'd planned, my three-year-old created an unpleasant confrontation and stubbornly went to bed without his treat rather than drink cocoa out of his favorite color cup. Who can figure?

I've completely given up trying to guess what new food my oldest son has decided not to like this week. And then there are clothes that were fine to wear last week but are suddenly banished to the back of a drawer never to be worn again except to avoid total nudity—on a cold winter day.

Friends with teenagers testify that the unpredictability doesn't necessarily fade as kids grow up either. One woman told me, "As a mother I've entered that realm of adolescence and I'm here to tell you: It's horrifying! My daughter has become so temperamental—almost manic-depressive at times. She is perfectly happy one minute and insane the next. I guess that's normal for adolescence."

Yes unpredictability is a normal part of motherhood. But that doesn't make it any less stressful.

Lack of Control

A related stressor that shows up in nearly all studies on job stress is lack of control. Whatever the job, from corporate executives to assembly-line workers, those factors over which workers have no control often create stress. The less control workers have in a situation, the more stress they feel.

One mother articulated her feelings on the subject this way: "I know a lot of people look at my job as a stay-at-home mom and envy me what they think is the opportunity to determine my own tasks and schedules. But the reality is: I have little control over my job. Most of what I do is determined by the needs, schedules, and expectations of my children or my husband. My time just is not my own."

"When you stay home with a baby," reported Martha, who has one infant and a six-year-old daughter, "you think, *As soon as she gets to sleep I'll do this or that. But the end of the day will come and it would seem she'd never been asleep for more than a few minutes at time. I could never get done what I planned.*"

In some ways, you have even less control over your time when kids get to be school-age. You have to get them to school and back and run them to a growing number of activities—music lessons, sports, Scouts.

"Now that my children are teenagers," said Darlene, who has two, "There are so many new things that seem totally out of my control. Such as dating relationships. When my daughter's heart is broken I can't just fix it. I feel the terrible stress of helplessness."

Though the out-of-control feelings last throughout motherhood, they often seem to intensify whenever a new baby arrives in the family. In the outside working world it's analogous to getting another boss to whom you're responsible. And office job stress studies will tell you, the more bosses a person has, the greater the potential for stress.

This lack-of-control stress sometimes seems stronger for a woman who has postponed motherhood. (The number of such women has multiplied in the past twenty-five years with the double-barrelled impact of effective birth control and feminism.) In taking time to establish our careers before having children, many of us have exercised control over our own lives as women, in ways that were not options for our mothers and grandmothers.

Women who leave other careers to begin motherhood experience a role change similar to retirement for men—with the need to adjust to similar losses and constraints.

This later adjustment to motherhood is then doubly tough, particularly on managerial women. As pointed out by Dr. Sirgay Sanger, co-author of *The Woman Who Works, The Parent Who*

Cares, "[They] are used to being in control at work, and, like all parents, have to come to terms with the fact that children aren't controllable; they're their own persons."

Even when we understand and accept the uncontrollable nature of children, even when we accept the fact that motherhood often requires us to subjugate our own wills and needs to those of the people we serve, surrendering control creates stress.

But it's not just children and their needs that cannot be controlled. Sometimes it's circumstances or a combination of factors over which a mother has no control.

One mother told me this story: "I was pregnant with our second child. My first was still a toddler. We were in the middle of redecorating our kitchen. I worked two part-time jobs. One night my husband, who's diabetic, had a serious insulin reaction while I was at work. And I remember thinking, *Who gets cared for first here?* I felt like there was no control over anything in my life."

Most mothers are usually at the hub of any and all activities or crises involving their family or any individual member of it. A mother is usually the person who takes primary responsibility for providing comfort and stability. Fair weather or foul, she's the family breakwater who tries to insure at least some sense of tranquility in the home harbor. She often takes the full brunt of those outside forces that threaten her loved ones. Control becomes an important goal, and lack of control becomes a constant fear she battles every day.

Actually, a lot of the stresses we'll be looking at in upcoming chapters often contribute to a mother's lack-of-control feelings. Lack of control is indeed a major job stress—for mothers as much as, or perhaps even more than, anyone else.

Complexity of the Job

Big-time jugglers always have a gimmick to wow the crowd. Apples and tennis balls are seldom enough. Flaming sticks provide photogenic drama. Juggling knives creates a sense of risk. But when my husband told me about the guy he'd seen on TV who juggled running chainsaws I thought that was too much. I wondered aloud, "How crazy would you have to be to risk (literally) life and limb like that?" Talk about job stress!

But the more I've thought about it, the more appropriate is the analogy I see here for mothers. Every one of us performs an impressive but stressful act—daily juggling needs, demands, desires, and dreams—thrown at us from all sides. Children, spouse, parents, friends, and employers are always contributing new elements, new challenges to our act. Though a slip-up in our daily performance isn't apt to result in a severed limb, we do face the stress of knowing our success or failure at balancing everything we juggle can have life-building or life-crippling impact on those we love most in life.

Just as a juggler's challenge grows with each ball or chainsaw added to the routine, a mother's juggling act gets tougher with each child coming into the family. The number of hours in the day never changes; you just have more ways to divide it up.

Audrey talked about the time after her second daughter was born: "Missy had always been such an independent little girl. But after Jessica came along she became very tender and easily hurt. She cried easily and got very impatient with me if I couldn't do what she needed immediately. Even though I understood what was going on, it was still stressful."

Often one person's needs conflict with another's—or with everyone's! Even as I struggled feverishly to finish up work on this book, my oldest son Andrew was in a local children's theatre production of Cinderella. My husband and I were thrilled that Andrew had won a part. We thought he could use an experience like this to bolster his self-esteem. We also saw it as a way for him to meet and make new friends after what was for Andrew a difficult interstate move. But with play practice several evenings a week, the entire family schedule often had to be changed. Pulling off a simple supper now required much logistical juggling. And that created stress, even in a temporary situation we knew would be over in a month.

The problem with a mother's juggling act is someone's always tossing in something new—usually when we're right in the middle of our carefully practiced routine. The temporary situations just keep changing until everything seems temporary—except the stress. To meet one person's need, we must toss something else a little higher and hope we can catch it again before everything comes crashing down around us.

Joyce, the mother of two teens, said: "Each child is so different. What you do with one might be wrong for the other. And as they grow older their needs change, too, and you're always wondering what your role is at this stage.

"In most jobs you have a job description you can look at and update. If it changes, it's written out and you know exactly what the expectations are. But a mother's job description changes every day. By the time you could ever get it written down, it'd be outdated."

And yet, the more complex, varied and changing any job description is, the more stress the task holds. So all in all, it's quite an act we mothers try to pull off. Some days I think juggling chainsaws would be a piece of cake.

Time Pressure

The fourth major job stress highlighted in my own chapter-opening anecdote also shows up in most of the job stress research. And that's time pressure.

"Mornings are the worst," one mother of three told me. "I can almost hear the clock ticking from the moment I climb out of bed until the kids walk out the door to school."

Every mother knows the feeling. I know I do. My K-Mart experience was all too typical. Sometimes I feel like a prisoner of time—with the clock my jailer, constantly prodding me along from one activity to the next. The biggest time pressure is that there are only twenty-four hours in a day—and there's invariably more to do than I can possibly fit in.

Every family has its own special times of stress. "Morning" is usually one of them. So, any mother who works outside the home can empathize with Audrey, who said: "Regardless of when I get up, something always happens and any extra time somehow disappears. Fortunately, I work in a job where I don't punch a clock, because by the time I get a baby and a kindergartner ready for the day, it seems impossible to get to work on time. I'm often so exhausted by the time I get there. I feel like the day ought to be over before it even gets started."

According to Harriet, weekends present a unique time stress for two-career mothers: "All week you look forward to the weekend. You think this weekend you will have time to clean the house, buy groceries, prepare good meals, maybe cook some ahead for next week, spend a lot of quality family time together, and get lots of rest. Ha. Ha. I'm often so tired and frustrated by all the things I planned and didn't get done, that I'm almost glad Monday morning when the weekend is behind me. The weekends are just never long enough to do everything you need to do, let alone want to do."

Then there are those very different, but all too frequent time stresses when the family schedule requires a mother to be in three places at once. (And two was usually more than even Clark Kent or Wonder Woman could manage.)

*   *   *

When you multiply the continuous time pressure by the complexity of the job and mix in a generous portion of unpredictability and strong lack-of-control feelings, you've got a potent recipe for motherhood stress right there. But there are lots of other stressful ingredients yet to add—as you'll see in the following chapters.

3

I Wasn't Ready for This!

Before I had children of my own, I learned a few lessons about job stress as the director of a day-care and nursery school. I watched that center grow from a staff of three part-time teachers and ten children to a staff of thirteen employees who were responsible for more than a hundred three- to five-year-olds. So I knew there was more to the business of caring for children than just "playing with kids all day."

In that job, I learned much about the unpredictable nature of small children. Daily I struggled to find new ways to control the uncontrollable in the face of constant change. And there were, of course, all sorts of time pressures—from the first of the month billings to the dreadful ringing of the phone at 5:30 in the morning—which I instantly knew meant I'd have to cover for the sick staff member who was scheduled to open up the center at 6:00.

There was always more to do than could be done. So I began each day by making out a to-do list. I would then prioritize it: "A" for things that needed to be done that day; "B" for things that could wait a day or so; "C" for things that could wait longer. These regular, specific goals could be accomplished if I worked hard enough or long enough or efficiently enough. And I felt a sense of accomplishment with each item I checked off my list.

In spite of the stress, I not only coped, I succeeded. My school grew; we had an excellent reputation. I had the affirmation of my bosses, my teachers, and the parents of the children in my school.

Having done all that, and having been responsible for the daily care of a hundred children, I expected the transition to motherhood to be a breeze. It took only one baby for me to realize I'd been wrong. Very wrong.

There were job stresses I never imagined.

The Significance of the Job

Ask any group of people to name the world's most stressful occupations and you can be sure "air traffic controllers" will make the list. Everyone recognizes stress in jobs requiring life-and-death judgments.

Ask the same group to list the name of the individual who holds the most stressful position in the world, and invariably someone will suggest the president of the United States. We have only to compare a president's picture at his inauguration with his visage when he leaves the White House after four or eight years for a quick measure of the stress that results from the burden of such power and responsibility.

We readily accept the fact that the seriousness or significance of any job adds to its stress. Yet we're slow to recognize the stress of motherhood—a job that comes with the humbling, sometimes staggering responsibility for the physical, emotional, social, and spiritual lives of our children.

Personally, as the mother of a large family, I can identify very readily with an air traffic controller. At night. In the fog. Without radar. Realizing I'm responsible for the safety and survival of all five of my charges landing at once. Knowing none of them has flown this route before.

Perhaps that's overstating my motherhood stress. A little.

But a friend of mine had this to say about her discovery of the stressful feelings of significance after her first child was born: "I'd been married for two years and I loved my husband Jeff very much. I thought he was the most wonderful person I'd ever known. Then we had our baby, Cindy. I won't say that the love I had for Jeff after that was any less, it just seemed so different. I knew that if I died, Jeff would be saddened by losing me, but he could get married again and his life would go on. However, I realized if something happened to me, Cindy's life could never be the same again. The loss of a mother is so traumatic; she would never be able to replace her mother. And that just terrified me, to think I might not be around for her when she grew up."

One of my favorite writers, *New York Times* columnist Anna Quindlen, writes poignantly of the great responsibility of motherhood. Despite all the books you read, all the advice you get when you're pregnant, Quindlen says, "No one ever tells you that what they are going to hand you in the hospital is power, whether you want it or not. . . .

"I am aghast to find myself in such a position of power over two people. Their father and I have them in thrall simply by having produced them. We have the power to make them feel good or bad about themselves, which is the greatest power in the world. Ours is not the only influence, but it is the earliest, the most ubiquitous and potentially the most pernicious. Lovers and friends will make them blossom and bleed, but they may move on to other lovers and friends. We are the only parents they will have.

"Sometimes one of them will put silky arms around my neck and stare deeply into my eyes like an elfin Svengali and say with full force of the heart, 'I love you.' My first reaction is to be drowned in happiness. My second is to think: *Don't mean it so much, don't feel it so deeply, don't let me have so much influence over you.* Of course I have no choice. Neither do they."

Such awesome power is a wonderful honor. But the heavy burden of such a responsibility can also be a terrible stress.

Obviously, fathers bear some of the weight when they assume their share of parenting responsibilities. (Single mothers have to feel immeasurably stressed.) But there's often a level of responsibility only a mother feels.

One woman I interviewed described it as *psychological responsibility.* "For example," she said, "who takes psychological responsibility for the children's health care? Who keeps track of immunizations? Knows how and decides when to get in touch with a doctor? Who decides what doctor to go to? Usually the mother.

"In our case," she went on, "it's allergy shots every week. I recently asked Bruce, 'Did I take Jimmy for his allergy shots last week?' I honestly couldn't remember. And Bruce replied, 'I don't know. I don't pay any attention to when you do that.'

"So I'm the one who carries around that mental file of information and schedules for allergy shots, checkups, doctors appointments, etc. Bruce couldn't tell you who the allergist is, who the ear doctor is—that's my job. It's in my file. They're invisible, not very measurable stresses."

Every mother can identify with this idea of assuming "psychological responsibility" for our children. Karla, the mother of a one-year-old son, said, "I wonder if I'm doing all the right things to help my son develop to his potential. Twenty years from now is someone going to look at him and say, 'If his mother would have done such and such, he'd have been fine'? Or he will take his SATs and they'll say, 'If only his mother had read to him more when he was a baby, he'd have done better.'"

Karla was assuming emotional responsibility for the development of her son. We all do it for our own children in a lot of different ways.

Before I had children I wondered if I'd ever hear my baby cry in the night. I slept so soundly an earthquake could have shaken our apartment building down around us and my husband would have had to awaken me to crawl out of the rubble. I worried that I might never qualify for a good mothering badge if ever my children needed nocturnal care.

The first night at home with our oldest son proved all my fears groundless. Every time Andrew wiggled a little hand or foot across the sheet in his crib, I awakened. At one point screeching tires and racing motors outside our apartment awakened me. Alarmed, I roused Gregg to ask what was going on. He laughed and said, "Nothing, the traffic sounds like that every night!" I'd just never heard it before. But I heard it every night thereafter— until we moved from that apartment. My lifelong sleeping patterns were permanently altered—all because I was a mother and had immediately assumed a sort of emotional responsibility I'd never known before.

I'd been so worried about my imagined lack of maternal instincts, that waking up and feeling emotional responsibility for my baby in the middle of the night seemed as reassuring to me as it was stressful. But that's not the case for everyone.

Recently I overheard a new mother talking about bringing her baby home from the hospital. "He was a full-term baby. No health problems. No hint of potential problems. But I'd read so much about SIDS (Sudden Infant Death Syndrome) that I'd lie in my bed all night, with his cradle on the floor next to me, and listen to him breathe, ready to jump up if he didn't take his next breath. I'd doze off in exhaustion from time to time, but the slightest noise would awaken me and I'd be wide awake again, afraid he'd stop breathing any moment."

This mother's feelings of emotional responsibility for her child quickly threatened her own health. She said, "After more than a week without ever really sleeping, I reached the end of my emotional rope. I was lying awake in the dark, listening, when I just broke down and prayed, 'Lord, if You're going to take him, take him. I can't go on like this.' And I finally went to sleep."

Most of us do eventually learn to relax a little. We all develop our own ways of coping with the feeling of responsibility.

Sometimes we even lose sight of the importance, the seriousness of our jobs as mothers. But inside, deep in our subconscious minds, we never are fully free of the weight of our awesome power in this eternally significant role we've been given in the lives of our children. So that stress is always there, too.

Inadequate Job Training

What makes it all the more stressful is that most of us come into motherhood woefully unprepared. Despite the immense responsibility of the job, no training is required of anyone, and there's little useful training available. There's no way for us to learn the most crucial elements of the job ahead of time.

Poor or insufficient training is a serious contributor to job

stress in any line of work. Government and business both recognize
the importance of training. Airline pilots have to log thousands of
flying hours before they can captain a Boeing 747. Teachers spend
years of study and at least a term of student teaching before they're
entrusted with a classroom of elementary students for six hours a
day. Even a McDonald's worker gets more formal training (complete with manuals and videotaped instructions) in how to prepare
hamburgers and French fries than the average new mother gets for
a job requiring life-and-death decisions (she's bestowed with the
power to control her child's entire world!).

Many mothers don't even know the basics when they start.
One woman, who worked seven years in her well-trained profession as a pharmacist before she had her first baby, said, "Being an
only child, I had never been around babies. I didn't know much
about them. I had babysat older children, but never babies. I
didn't know how to give a baby a bath, how to clean their little
noses out, how to change a diaper, or any of the other basic
day-to-day-you-got-to-know-this stuff."

Experiences like this woman's are not at all unusual. And
while all of us as mothers have to pick up some of the basics in
trial-and-error, on-the-job training, by the time we begin to feel
comfortable with the daily challenges, things have changed.

A friend lamented, "When you finally feel like you know
what you're doing with an infant, he's a toddler. By the time you
get a handle on your preschooler, she's in grade school. Then it's
junior high, and *no one* is prepared for adolescence. Everything
keeps changing so you never get a chance to be the perfect
mother."

Unrealistic Expectations

The goal many of us have, to be "the perfect mother,"
appears all the more worthy considering the high stakes of our
task, and all the more unattainable as we learn how unprepared
we are for the challenges—and even more so when we discover
the job's so complex no amount of training could ever be
enough, anyway.

In other jobs, perfection is more readily reachable. You could type a perfect letter, deliver a perfect speech, or pull off a perfect business deal. But a mother can't measure perfection by any one set of criteria. There's no one achievement by which to measure success. And if there were, you couldn't really know for twenty-one years—or maybe more.

Yet we all seem to come into motherhood holding tight to our own idealistic images of what being the perfect mother will be like.

"Before my first baby was born," confessed Alice, a woman in her late twenties, "I thought I had life as a mother planned. I'd clean house in the morning before the baby awakened. Then we'd go for an hour walk every morning. We'd do all these stimulating, interesting things together each day. And we'd be sitting there, smiling in the evening when Daddy got home. But it doesn't work that way.

"I thought I would manage because I've always been an organized person. But motherhood is not, at least in the first year, organized."

I could have told her, based on my own experience, the first ten years aren't organized! And I doubt I'll say any different after eighteen or twenty years.

Yet her comments suggest an explanation as to why the unattainable expectations we hold for ourselves as mothers become a major stress. At least in part it's because many of the skills that can bring real success in our other jobs don't transfer very well into motherhood. As Alice quickly discovered, neither planning nor organizing, two basic strategies that can spell success in any number of jobs, can be counted on to assure success as a mother.

And my old stand-by as a day-care director, the prioritized to-do list, isn't much better.

Unclear Priorities

It's not that a to-do list doesn't have any value. Many mothers can relate to what one mother of four said, "I'm always trying to catch my breath. Without my to-do list I can't even keep track of what I'm behind on."

What may not have come as any surprise to our mothers—but genuinely surprises many of us today—is the discovery that we can't schedule the needs of children and families like we juggle appointments in a business day.

Something happens. Your sixteen-year-old daughter calls to say the station wagon just stalled in the middle of a downtown street and she doesn't know where to have it towed or how to get home. Or your fifth-grader announces that tomorrow is the last day to turn in the big science paper he's been diligently working on for a month—and he's just found out he has to use one more reference book from the public library on the other side of town.

Unpredictability strikes again. And when it does, all the priorities on the to-do list change. Or the list gets discarded altogether.

I remember the first birthday party invitation for my oldest son, Andrew. He was three years old and so excited. We called his friend's mother to R.S.V.P. I wrote it on the kitchen calendar. We talked about it early in the week. I let Andrew pick out a present to take. Party plans were a big priority.

Then the night before the party, Andrew's younger brother, Matthew, woke up crying with a fever. I didn't get a decent night's sleep. It seemed all I could do just to get breakfast on the table by mid-morning. Lunch was late. But I did manage to get both kids in the car for a drive to the drugstore to pick up a prescription for Matthew. It wasn't till I was driving home and glanced at my watch to see it said 2:30, that I finally remembered the party which had started at 2!

We raced home. Hurriedly I wrapped the present, dressed Andrew in clean clothes and rushed to get him to the party just twenty minutes before it ended. I felt so bad. So stupid. So guilty.

But I've talked to many mothers who've had similar experiences. One priority suddenly takes precedence and everything else grinds to a halt. One of the kids gets sick and that's suddenly the focus of your entire world; you don't even think to look at a calendar. The rest of the world's time ceases to exist.

The other problem, besides suddenly changing priorities, is that many of the tasks of motherhood aren't easily prioritized. It's no longer a simple matter for me to begin each morning by looking at my to-do list and deciding this is an A priority, that's a B, and there is a C.

I often find that the most menial, least significant task (let's say laundering the kids' clothes) absolutely has to be done today, while a much more meaningful priority (such as taking my three-year-old to the library and checking out some new books to read together) could be put off forever. So often when it comes to deciding my priorities as a mother, I'm faced with a choice between the most urgent and the most significant.

Having to make such a no-win choice is stressful in itself. Whichever decision you make then results in frustration or guilt, or both.

For example, I had a teething baby yesterday who wanted to be held the entire time he was awake. I could have let him cry for a while and finished more of my laundry. Instead I chose to make comforting my baby my highest priority for the day. But not without cost. This morning I had to rummage through a basket of dirty clothes to find the cleanest long-sleeved shirt and corduroy pants for Andrew to wear to school.

The guilt and frustration we experience, whether the result of conflicting priorities, our own unrealistic expectations, or inadequate preparation for such a responsible job, can themselves become motherhood stresses.

And the number of potential stressors just keeps adding up.

4

Somebody Tell Me, How Am I Doing?

The ultrasound technician was grinning!

"I wasn't prepared for that reaction," remembers Marlene. "All day long I'd been afraid I was having a miscarriage."

She wasn't expecting to hear his words, either: "There are three."

"Three what?" she asked.

"Three babies!" the technician said.

Marlene began to cry with relief as the man explained that the bleeding which had begun that morning was a natural result of three fetuses simultaneously attaching to the uterine wall. "Can my husband come in?" she asked.

"Only if he doesn't faint," the technician replied.

"I think he was serious," Marlene says, looking back. "He had one patient lying on the table crying; he didn't want another one passed out on the floor."

When a nurse walked Marlene's husband, Tim, into the ultrasound room he wasn't sure how to react. His wife was crying, but the technician was still grinning.

"We're going to have three!" Marlene announced.

"Three what?" Tim asked.

"Three babies!"

"No!" Tim responded. "You're kidding!"

With that exciting news, Marlene's and Tim's lives were

instantly changed. Her doctor advised Marlene to quit her job immediately and stay off her feet for the next seven months or risk losing the babies. So while Marlene endured an extended period of imposed inactivity, Tim took on all the household duties.

There were other pressures as well. "There was so much to worry about," Marlene says. "First, of course, was the babies' health. We knew the chances of carrying and delivering three healthy babies were not good. On top of that was our financial situation. Even with insurance, the cost of having three babies would be high. The place we were renting wasn't big enough for three babies. Either we had to start working on all the plans to build a home or buy one. And we were suddenly reduced to one income months before we'd expected."

Despite the stress of the pregnancy, Marlene optimistically faced the challenge ahead. When asked if she felt ready for triplets she honestly and naively replied, "I think so. Because twins seem like they would be a breeze, and four would be one too many."

Reality finally arrived in the form of three tiny infants—two girls and a boy—the biggest, 3 lbs. 14 oz. and the smallest, 2 lbs. 14 oz. A month after their births, all three babies were strong enough to go home with Marlene and Tim. And then the true challenge began.

Thirty diapers a day needed to be changed. Formula was prepared by the gallon. Thirty bottles at a time were sterilized, filled and stored in the refrigerator for daily use. All three babies had to be fed at three-hour intervals around the clock. And so on and on and on.

Visitors to Marlene and Tim's home felt as if they had walked into a baby factory. The workload proved enormous.

But Marlene and Tim gladly devoted themselves to their children. "We had to cooperate like never before, just to cope with the daily routine," Marlene remembers. "We were almost *forced* to grow as a couple. We prayed more together about our worries. And we learned to communicate our feelings better as we shared our fears.

"We didn't have much time or energy to devote to our own relationship, but neither of us seemed to notice or mind all that much. We loved the kids so much and we knew they wouldn't be tiny forever. We just accepted the fact that they needed to be the focus of our lives for the next few years."

But after almost three years, things began to change. As the children graduated from diapers and their care became a little less demanding, Tim decided to start night school at a nearby police reserve academy and also began doing part-time police work a couple nights a week.

Marlene can't say for sure what triggered the crisis. Tim's evenings away from home no doubt contributed to the problem. It was winter, so the whole family felt bored and cooped up. And the accumulated effect of three-and-a-half very stressful years finally took its toll.

"I felt so discouraged," Marlene admits. "I had worked so hard to be a great mother, a great wife, a great housekeeper. Yet I felt like a total failure. In all my other jobs my hard work had always paid off with promotions or some pat on the back. There was always some measure of success and some visible reward.

"I just didn't have that anymore. Doing a good job of taking care of my children was just expected. Even when I did something extra like waxing the floor or cooking a special meal, Tim didn't seem to notice. I began to wonder if he loved me as he had before.

"I'd seen other people go through what I felt," says Marlene. "But I'd never experienced depression myself."

*　*　*

Any mother who remembers how one utterly helpless newborn threw her entire known world into anarchy can hardly begin to imagine the implications of triplets. Total dependency times three has to equal a great deal of motherhood stress.

But the primary reason I tell Marlene and Tim's story here is that it so clearly illustrates the significance of yet another major factor in job stress—feedback.

Inadequate Feedback

Study after study has proved that (1) the amount, (2) the tone (positive or negative), and (3) the timing of feedback a person gets in any job directly affects the amount of job stress that worker experiences. Too often, mothers lose out on all three counts. Even women like Marlene, married to sensitive and helpful husbands like Tim, can feel that no one notices what they are doing or if they're doing anything at all.

As Connie, mother of three gradeschoolers pointed out: "You don't get clear feedback as a mother until your kids are grown and gone away. There's no periodic evaluation, no yearly reviews to say, 'You're doing a good job.' And it's hard to sit back and evaluate yourself on the job you're doing."

Another mom with two boys (ages nine and six) said, "I recently realized I don't hear any specific feedback from my husband—positive or negative—about what kind of a mother I am. I decided I need that. But when I told my husband he acted a little surprised. He said sure, he thought I was a good mother. But that wasn't very meaningful feedback. Mostly he seemed at a loss to know what to say. And that made me wonder if he doesn't say anything because he doesn't know how to rank me."

This woman may be right. Men have a pretty limited picture of motherhood. They saw their own mothers and now they see their children's mother. But most of them learned shortly after they said, "I do," that it's not a good idea to compare the two—at least not out loud. So the average husband, without much of a basis for meaningful feedback, says little or nothing positive about his wife's mothering. And the resulting absence of positive feedback adds to job stress for a mother, just as it does in any other job.

Negative Feedback

However, the stress created by inadequate positive feedback may be less than the stress resulting from insensitive and/or negative feedback. An unfortunate number of mothers get that, too.

One mother with a two-year-old boy gave this example:

"I'd have a long list of things that needed doing. Then Joey would wake up fussing with a cold and want to be held all day. I'd decide to stay home rather than expose him to other kids. But whenever I'd sit him down with toys and try to do something else, he'd fuss and I'd hold him again. Before I knew it the day would be gone and my husband Joe would walk in from work and ask, 'Did you get by the dry cleaners today?'

"'Nooo,' I'd growl. Now he *has* learned not ever to ask, 'What did you do today?'"

Unfortunately, some husbands haven't learned that lesson yet. Even if you've been at your most productive and crossed off everything on your to-do list for today *and* tomorrow, "What did you do today?" can sound like, "I don't see a thing you've accomplished"—whether he means that or not. And if you've had one of those days when you have yet to finish job one, that innocent query can sound to an already discouraged mother like the final judgment of the gods ringing down from the heavens. Either way, it's negative feedback on the job done that day.

What's harder on the stress level is the husband who is downright critical. I talked to some mothers whose spouses were.

A mother of two preschoolers told me: "Henry would come home from work, pick up the baby and say, 'Karen's diaper is wet. Haven't you changed her today?' Of course, I had—about eight or ten times. But there was no acknowledgment of that. Just an accusing question. It was that way with everything, 'Why did you get the kids those shoes?' or 'You dressed Timmy in that?'

"I couldn't even sweep the kitchen floor right! For a long time the criticism made me angry. But eventually I began believing it and wondering if I was capable of doing anything right."

Obviously, this woman's case is an extreme example. But it doesn't take much negative feedback to undermine a mother's (or any other worker's) self-esteem. Sometimes just a lack of *positive* feedback can do the same thing.

And when a mother isn't getting meaningful positive feedback from her husband, it means she isn't getting it from the people who matter most. It's not as if a six-year-old is going to walk up to her, give her a warm hug and say, "Mom, I think you've been doing an especially wonderful job of mothering me this week."

Feedback from Peers

Mothers often don't even have that source of feedback most jobs offer—the friendly feedback you get from co-workers and colleagues working at the next desk or down the hall. Stay-at-home mothers with tiny children can feel an especially intense sense of isolation from the rest of the world.

"Nothing I ever read about pregnancy, childbirth or motherhood prepared me for the loneliness of my little girl's first year," said Tamara, a mother of one toddler. "I was alone so much of the time. Alone without the freedom to go that I'd always had. While I loved my daughter and I loved so many things about being a mom, I sometimes felt as if I was in solitary confinement."

Another mother of three preschoolers lamented: "Sometimes I go for days without a meaningful conversation. And you can only take so much Dr. Seuss!"

But this isolation affects more than those mothers at home with young children. One mother with three teenagers said, "Last week in Sunday school I mentioned how guilty I'd felt recently for screaming so much at my kids. When no one said anything in response, I figured I must be the only screamer. I felt very alone."

Even mothers who have jobs outside the home and get positive feedback at the office don't usually get feedback about their mothering. And then the contrast between their other work and their mother-work seems to suggest, "You're doing a good job at the office, but not so good as a mother."

When we don't get the emotional support of positive feedback from our mothering peers, we naturally feel isolated. And feeling "alone" in any job adds to stress.

Feedback from Others

Recently at church I was turtle-ing down the stairs behind my three-year-old Benjamin, talking with him as we went. We finally reached the bottom of the steps to be greeted by the smiling face of an older woman who teaches in the Sunday school preschool department. "You seem like such a good mother," she said, "You're being so patient with Benjamin."

Actually patience is one of those virtues I'm always praying for more of as a mother. I can get so impatient sometimes. But I'm consciously working at it. So that positive comment on my patience brightened my whole day.

In fact, that seemingly incidental feedback made such a positive impact on my feelings that it struck me how seldom I ever hear encouragement like that. And how crucial positive feedback actually can be.

I'm fortunate that my own parents and my in-laws say encouraging things about my mothering. But many women don't even have that.

"I don't get any feedback at all from my mother or mother-in-law," said one mother of two young boys. "Which I can only assume means they think I'm doing okay. Because I got more feedback when they were infants and some of that was negative. 'When are you going to potty-train him?' and that kind of thing."

A mother of eight- and ten-year old sons told me: "I dread every visit with my parents. They believe our approach to child-rearing is completely wrong. For example, they think I should dish out everything onto the boys' plates—the amount I think they should eat. And that I should make them sit at the table until they finish every bite I serve them. They think I should pick out the clothes the boys wear every morning. They complain that by giving the boys 'too many choices' we're guaranteeing their rebellion as teenagers and losing our best chance to teach them the meaning of discipline.

"My husband and I completely disagree with my parents. We're actually pretty strict parents. But we're convinced that by giving our boys limited choices, we're encouraging responsible decision-making skills they'll need growing up.

"Even so, even though I firmly believe my parents are off-base in their opinions, their judgment hurts. And every time we get together it creates a great deal of tension for me."

Parents aren't the only people whose negative feedback can create stress. One mother, who has chosen to take a few years out of her nursing profession to be at home with her two grade-school-age girls, said this about her colleagues' reactions: "Friends call me from the hospital and pressure me to come back to work. They tell me they are short-staffed, they're overworked, and the patients aren't getting the care they need. They say, 'How can you stay at home when you have skills that are needed?'

"I believe I'm doing what is right for myself and my children at this point. But my friends tell me I'm making a big mistake. They make me feel guilty."

Another mother (a pharmacist with a toddler) who has opted to return to work has gotten the opposite feedback. She said, "My husband wanted me to go back to work so I wouldn't fall behind in my field. But the church we attended felt that a mother's place was in the home and that was final. Even though I found a wonderful person who would babysit right in our home, a lot of people were saying, 'You're leaving your baby too soon. You should be staying at home.' Some speakers at our church even blamed a lot of the problems in the world on the fact that mothers go out and work.

"We finally found another church. It hurt too much knowing so many people thought I was wrong in what I did."

It seems every mother has someone who thinks she can't possibly be as good a mother as she ought to be if she's working outside the home. And every mother has someone in her life who thinks she ought to pursue other work to earn money or realize her personal potential. So whatever choice we make, we're going to get negative feedback. And that only adds to any stress we already feel.

Society's Feedback —a Matter of Status

Our entire culture—our government, our churches, and almost every individual in our society—says it values mothers. Yet the lack of status bestowed on motherhood often says otherwise.

Last year Jan, mother of two school-aged children, volunteered at her church to head up a new program—a support group for adult children of aging parents. She developed a plan for the group, planned meetings, arranged for speakers, etc. She spent time reading up on the subject, tracking down resources and recruiting people for the group. She found her effort time-consuming, challenging, and interesting.

One day her fifth-grade daughter's teacher called to say, "Jill tells me you don't do anything, uh, I mean you don't work."

"I work at home," Jan told her.

"Oh, I understand that," the teacher assured her. "It's just that we need someone like you to be room mother."

The entire attitude was, "Since you don't work, you must have time to do this."

The same woman told about going to her husband's high school reunion: "This lady walked up to me, held out her hand in greeting, and said, 'Your name is Jan and you don't do anything, do you?' She caught herself and added, 'Oh, that's not what I meant—you don't work outside the home.' And I found out this is another at-home mom, too!"

Melissa, a mother with two preschoolers, who quit working as an accountant when her second child was born, speaks of telling comments from professional friends who say: "It must be nice to be home and have all that time."

Comments like these reflect the value often placed on mothering. Other times it's reflected in what's not said.

For example, when I meet new people and answer their questions about what work I do by saying "I teach college" or "I'm writing a book right now," they are always impressed. They often have numerous questions to ask. But when I say, "I'm the mother of five children"—the job that consumes most of my time and energy—they seldom think of anything to ask me.

So I can identify with the mother who confessed: "I miss the acceptance, the approval and the self-respect I found in pursuing a career."

But it's not just what people say or don't say that reminds me of my low status as a mother. Often it's something more subtle that speaks just as clearly.

For example, a few weeks ago I took all five of my children to the library to enroll them in a new reading incentive program I'd read about in the newspaper. The children picked out four books apiece and we went to the circulation desk to inquire about the sign-up procedure for the new program. I stood and watched as the librarian smiled and chatted warmly with the patrons in front of me—a father with a five-year-old daughter and an elderly woman, obviously a grandmother, and her little grandson. Then came my turn.

But as the young male librarian looked up at me, with a baby in my arms and four kids behind me, his smile vanished. A cool businesslike look replaced it. No, I couldn't register my children today. The program started tomorrow. And he turned away before I could ask my next question.

I asked it anyway. In all, I had four questions to ask about the children's book club. Each question was answered as curtly as possible, then he'd turn back to other work before I'd ask the next. So I felt as if I were interrupting him four times.

While his demeanor had been so positive, so personally respectful of the father and grandmother who'd each brought a child to the library, he seemed to have better things to do than talk to "just a mother."

As I listened to the condescending tone with which he answered my questions I thought to myself, *What if I could somehow work into this conversation the fact that I'm currently writing a book about motherhood stress that's scheduled for publication in a few months? Librarians respect authors. Would that rate me a smile and a few graciously answered questions?*

I don't for a moment believe that man was deliberately writing me off as "just a mother." But that's what his actions said to me. And like most mothers, I've had similar experiences often enough to believe it was a reflection of my lack of status in his eyes.

A little different example:

Martha, a divorced mother of two grade-school kids, worked as an office manager for a local insurance agency. When she started the job she called every afternoon after school to make sure her children were home and okay; they also knew they could call her if they needed her. But Martha soon realized her boss's unspoken policy didn't allow for such intrusions into the work day, so she surreptitiously placed her daily call. But after twice experiencing her employer's disfavor, she eventually had to discontinue her own calls and instruct her children not to call her at the office unless there was a dire emergency. "The job was a good one," she said. "And I got good recognition and reward for what I did. But it was like my being a mother was of no importance at all."

Mothers get that same message in a lot of ways. And if you think I've overstating the low status our society places on motherhood, think again. Consider the fact that day-care workers with whom we entrust the lives of our children are often paid minimum wage or little more. Think about the lack of consideration given women returning to the work force after taking time out to raise their children. Ask yourself why more companies don't offer protected or longer maternity leaves. What all this says is that mothers still don't have the high status in our culture that everyone is so quick to say we deserve. And low status shows up on many studies as a major job stress.

Finally, one more job stress that's often lumped together with low status is low pay. But at least a paycheck, even a small one, is feedback that says a person's work has some value. And we don't even get that for our mothering. In a society where everyone wants to be paid what he or she is worth, it's easy for mothers to feel their work isn't valued.

The combination of the positive feedback mothers don't get and the negative feedback we do receive can have a potentially devastating impact on self-esteem. Study after study shows a direct relationship between self-esteem and job stress. When a person's self-esteem plummets, the stress level in any job goes up.

5

Everyone Knows My Job

Around the lunch table sat eight mothers of small children. We'd just finished a mother's support group meeting and had stayed to share a salad meal together and visit.

The conversation turned, as it almost always does, to children and mothering issues. We discussed children's nightmares and children climbing into bed with parents in the middle of the night.

Sandy, a mother of two preschoolers, expressed her frustration with an approach advocated by the writer of a recent article in a major national parenting magazine. This author, a pediatrician, had insisted the only way to deal with children seeking middle-of-the-night sanctuary in a parent's bed was to put the child—frightened or not—back into his own bed immediately and make him stay there.

"I just can't do that!" Sandy exclaimed. "When Jeremy wants comfort, I want to comfort him. And I don't really mind him in bed with us. Yet that doctor made me feel like I ought to mind it."

Our table talk instantly broadened to the subject of parenting advice—both books and magazines.

"I just don't read that stuff anymore," one mother commented.

"The best thing to do is forget all that advice and go with your instincts," another added.

43

"I used to read that magazine from cover to cover after Jeremy was born. I'd even cut out articles and file them," Sandy said. Then she added hesitantly, "But . . . when Jori came along, I hated reading it. There were all these articles, all these things they said I should be doing with her. And all I could think was: *I didn't do any of those things with Jeremy! Now he is four years old and it's too late!*

"I finally cancelled my subscription. I got so discouraged reading about all the things I wasn't doing that I ought to be doing—or at least doing differently. I just wanted to relax and enjoy being a mother."

In the next minute or so, every mother around the table confessed that she, too, had stopped taking that magazine for the same reason. And as we all laughed about it, I think each one of us felt a sense of relief to know we weren't alone.

*   *   *

While most mothers experience a sad lack of constructive feedback on the mothering job they're doing, there seems to be no end to the advice and direction being given to us as mothers. Just browse through the parenting section of any bookstore or thumb through any of the national women's magazines. The sheer volume and variety of the advice in print is mind-boggling.

You can find a wealth of wisdom in all those printed pages out there; I'm certainly not declaring a blanket condemnation of all parenting books and articles. In fact, the printed resources available to mothers today are often reassuring and helpful. But . . . .

What all that parenting advice doesn't tell us, what all those experts aren't saying, is: Mothering is more of a fly-by-the-seat-of-your-pants madcap adventure than it is a carefully plotted and provisioned scientific expedition. For all the reasons we've already talked about here—unpredictability, lack of control, and many of the other stresses of the job—we have to react to today's demands far more often than we can contemplate tomorrow's itinerary.

One mother of two children likened it to "a bumper car ride at the fair. Every time you turn around something else hits you from another direction. You're always having to take care of this emergency or solve that problem." What's fun for a few minutes at the fair becomes a tough way to live all of life.

Consequently, there's a limit to how much all that advice actually helps. Some broad principles can offer reassuring parameters to keep our parenting voyage moving safely and surely in the right general direction. And occasionally some specific how-to suggestion will come as the perfect solution for this mother and this child and this situation. When that happens the advice can seem invaluable.

But there comes a point, and all the mothers eating lunch together that day had reached it, when all the advice and direction adds more stress than it relieves, because it can't account for your specific situation or the bumps you're feeling on any given day. And unfortunately, not all advice (and the stress it may cause) can be dealt with as easily as cancelling a magazine subscription.

Sometimes It's Relative

Naturally, the people who love mothers most and know them best are often the most free with advice. And it frequently adds to the stress level.

Lorraine, mother of two preschoolers, told me: "If anybody ever needed church, it's us by the time we can get there. My five-year-old hates wearing Sunday pants and shoes. So he whines and complains from the time he gets up. And that only slows us down in the race with the clock.

"So my husband says, 'Well, you know the smart thing to do would be for you to set everyone's clothes out on Saturday night.' Right. I should set the clothes out . . . And I'm thinking *Unhuh. That's easy for you to say when you're watching a ball game or something on TV and trying to relax on Saturday night.* Somehow, his Sunday morning advice doesn't always set well with me."

Lynn, another mother with three small children, said: "I've spent most of the past five years either pregnant or nursing babies. As a result, I'm constantly worn out. And a lot of days I feel tied down.

"One day a few months ago, when our youngest, Andrea, was only a couple of months old, I unloaded on Bill [her husband]. I told him I was tired of feeling tired and trapped. I could never get away. I never had any time to myself, and on and on.

"His reaction was, 'Then why not quit breast feeding? You'd be able to get away from home for a while, and I could take care of Andrea. I could get up with her in the middle of the night, and you could get more rest.'

"I was so upset I exploded: 'You don't understand! I don't really want to stop nursing. I know I'm tired and this isn't going to last forever. I realize this is just the stage of life we're in right now, and I know it will get better. So I don't want your advice! I just want to tell you what I'm feeling right now. I just want you to listen!'"

Sometimes it's not so much a husband's direct advice which adds to motherhood stress, but rather the expectations you know he has about what you should be doing. Betsy, a nurse with three children, gave a good example. "One of the kids was sick. He'd had a slight fever the night before, but it was gone by morning. All my nurse's training told me I shouldn't expose him to other kids for twenty-four hours after a fever. So my inclination was to keep him home from school. But I felt conflicting pressure from my husband whose mother had always sent kids to school dead or alive. I knew his attitude was, *Never miss school unless absolutely necessary*. So I sent my son and felt terrible about it."

And of course husbands aren't the only ones with conflicting expectations and a ready supply of advice that creates more stress than it relieves. There are always mothers of mothers. And in-laws.

Mary, the mother of two grade-schoolers and a three-year-old, told me: "I love my mother dearly. We enjoy each other's company. She's loving and generous to me and my family in so many ways. But when she calls and says, 'I'm thinking of driving up to see you this weekend, got any special plans?' I always feel a little dread. Because I know I'll have to blitz the house from top to bottom between now and Friday.

"Even then, she'll notice a half-dozen things that haven't

been done around the house and lovingly say, 'Let me polish this for you,' or 'As long as I'm here, let me clean your oven for you.' She means well, but everything she offers to do around the house seems like a little judgment against me for not having done it.

"On the one hand she says she understands that I work and can't do everything. But on the other hand, she's says, 'You know, if you'd do that this way you could . . . .' Even where her advice is good, it adds pressure I don't want—and don't need."

Friendly Advice

Well-meaning friends can add to the stress with their own "helpful" advice. I remember talking at church to a young mother of two preschoolers about my frustration with keeping my house presentable. "Oh," she said, obviously glad to share her advice on this subject, "I've found the secret is keeping a strict schedule. I like to have the house clean for the weekend, so I straighten up and do my housework every Thursday."

I wanted to say something sarcastic like, "So do I. And then again on Friday and Saturday and all the other days of the week." But I bit my tongue. Even though I didn't consider her advice very realistic, I wondered what it was she did that I didn't do which made housework so simple for her.

Then I went to her house. It was indeed clean and neat; her system worked—though I couldn't imagine how. Until I'd been there for two hours and realized her three-year-old daughter had sat at our feet passively playing with the same little toy the entire time. Then my four-year-old came walking down the hall with her husband's guitar (which had been sitting on a chair in the master bedroom). I was concerned enough to jump to my feet and take the expensive instrument. But I wasn't prepared for my friend's reaction. She was aghast at my son's behavior. "My children have never gone in our bedroom without permission," she said, obviously thinking there was something wrong with any mother's child who would.

I went home a short while after that, better understanding how she could "Just do housework on Thursdays"—and reminding myself that some advice is absolutely worthless! For any advice to work, it has to fit my family, my personal style, the personality of my children and a whole lot more. Trying to force a friend's advice to fit my mothering style can sometimes result in frustration and added stress.

Even Stranger Advice

Sometimes people you don't even know feel free to offer advice—especially if they see you with a baby.

I remember taking my first son grocery shopping when he was only a few months old. I'd placed his infant seat carefully in the shopping cart, facing toward me so I could watch him and talk to him as we wheeled through the store. At one point I stopped in a crowded produce aisle and stepped up beside my cart to examine some clusters of seedless grapes. My cart was right beside me, almost against my leg as I turned and looked for the prettiest bunches.

I'd been standing there for only a few seconds when a white-haired, sophisticated gentleman touched me lightly on the arm and said, "You know, dear, you shouldn't turn your back on your baby for even a second in this grocery store. You never know what might happen." Then he nodded politely and walked away. My first reaction was instant guilt for being such an inadequate mother. I felt a sudden performance stress and I hadn't even realized I was performing. Then the frustration descended: "Can't I even look at grapes for thirty seconds without neglecting my baby?"

Ten years have passed and I can still see that elderly man's kindly face and feel the stinging rebuke of his words. It was the first time I remember getting unsolicited mothering suggestions from a total stranger; but it was by no means the last.

Unwanted Medical Attention

A friend of mine with a nine-month-old baby happened to mention to her pediatrician during a routine, well-baby checkup that she had a hard time getting her little girl to take her liquid vitamin supplement—she always tried to spit it out.

"Just mix it in her cereal," the doctor said.

"I've offered her cereal, but she doesn't seem to want solids," my friend told him.

"You're still nursing that baby, aren't you?" the doctor asked accusingly.

"Well, sure . . ."

"Then you ought to wean her right away," he replied. "Get her on solid food."

My friend, who wasn't ready to wean her baby and hadn't seen any need to, responded: "If you think there's a problem, let's do a hemoglobin test."

"Oh, no!" the doctor told her. "I can tell by looking at her she's perfectly healthy—not anemic. But you need to get her on solid foods."

"I cried all the way home from that doctor's appointment," my friend told me. "I felt I was doing what was best for my baby. But my doctor made me feel like I'd been a neglectful mother."

I have questions about any doctor who looks at a healthy infant and decides he has a better idea than God did for meeting that baby's basic nutritional needs. (But that's another subject.) My point here is that people in the medical profession often impose unnecessary stress on mothers with their professional opinions.

Janice, another mother with eight- and five-year-old boys, told me: "I'm the one who takes the boys to the dentist. So I'm the one who gets the guilt trip when the dentist says, 'You should really be flossing your children's teeth for them every day. They're not old enough to do it properly themselves.'

"Give me a break! I'm sorry, but I feel like I'm doing pretty well if I get them in the bathroom with a toothbrush that has toothpaste on it. And the dentist tells me every time we see him that I ought to be flossing their teeth?

"I'm not sure my dentist lives in the real world. In fact, I'm about to switch dentists because it's driving me nuts!"

I'm sure her dentist has no intention of adding to this mother's job stress level. But he does.

And the Bible Says . . .

When Andrew and Matthew were little, I listened to one of my first Mother's Day sermons as a mother. In extolling the virtues of motherhood, the minister told the story of his mother who always ate the chicken backs, letting her children eat the better pieces of the chicken. He then moved on to tell the story of a "fine Christian mother" who kept her home spotlessly clean as a labor of love for her family; she viewed scrubbing the family toilets as a spiritually uplifting task. The point of the sermon seemed to be that, in order for me to be a "fine, Christian mother" I should eat chicken backs and keep my toilets spotlessly clean.

As he spoke, I could see, in my mind's eye, the overflowing diaper pail in our bathroom. And all I could think was, *Am I a bad mother simply because I've never eaten a chicken back? Is something spiritually wrong with me because I do not feel "spiritual" about cleaning the toilet?*

Let me quickly say that my personal Christian faith is of utmost importance to me. So is the guidance and fellowship I get from my church. And I wholeheartedly believe in the Bible as God's basic guidebook for living. So I depend on, and value, the spiritual input I seek and receive in my faith—as a mother and as a person.

And I'd also add that the Christian church in North America is doing far more for mothers and families (through day-care, mothers'-day-out ministries, shelters for battered or homeless mothers, and much more) than our secular society ever seems to recognize. I find much truth and wisdom in what the church and Christian leaders are saying and writing today about the primary importance of family in God's plan for our world.

But I think our Christian community needs to realize that even the unrealistic ideals of motherhood and family we sometimes espouse as "spiritual" can seem like one more stress on already stress-sensitive mothers. *I have all these expectations; now it's my church or my minister saying I need to do this.*

*   *   *

Each piece of advice, whether it's sought or unsolicited, practical or worthless, adds one more element to a mother's job description. The bigger and more complex the job description (whatever the profession), the more stress.

6

All That Work

One mother of four had this to say about the requirements of motherhood:

"I thought a lot about the physical demands last winter because we were sick so much. And of course, when I was sick I also had sick children. I did take it easy and tried to lie on the couch a lot. And my family was pretty understanding. But still, when they needed something, I was the one who had to get up and get it.

"And then there's the matter of sleep. Our eleven-year-old walks in her sleep. Our eight-year-old gets growing pains that wake him in the night. And the four-year-old we adopted a couple years ago is just now starting to sleep through the night. For the longest time she'd awaken almost every night screaming and wanting to be held.

"When you have your first baby you gear yourself up and think, *I'm probably not going to get a full night's sleep for three or four months.* You assume that when your child gets a little older, she'll start sleeping through the night. But ours haven't. In fact, we've rarely gotten a full night's sleep—for sixteen years now! And now we have a teenager which means some weekends we're waiting up for her until midnight.

"One of these days, we've got to get some sleep!"

Physical Demands

Any jobs out there in the workplace with regular mandatory night-time hours, no overtime compensation, and no sick leave, would seem ripe for unionism. They'd certainly be considered stressful, physically demanding jobs. So why isn't motherhood? After all, lack of sleep and a you-can't-call-in-sick policy are only a small part of the physical demands on mothers.

Since wives and mothers often rely on husbands and fathers to help with physical challenges such as opening stubborn pickle jars and hauling bulky bags of grass clippings to the curb on trash day, the strength and energy we expend in the course of our routine tasks often goes unrecognized. But think for a minute of all the hauling and lifting a mother does every week—every day. With just the clothesbaskets and grocery sacks we tote (often up and down stairs), it's a wonder more mothers don't have Arnold Schwartzeneggar's biceps. And that's just for laundry, cooking, and kitchen chores.

There's a lot of other strenuous exercise involved in routine housework. Just removing wet sheets and remaking a top bunk bed with dry, fresh linen can provide a rigorous aerobic workout. Scrubbing, washing, bending, lifting, rearranging, and much more demand peak physical effort. Often, even the physical effort required for decorating and redecorating (painting, wallpapering, etc.) comes from mothers.

And we haven't yet mentioned the physical demands of caring for children. Because men have no physical parallels to the female functions in pregnancy, birth, and nursing, there's a lack of recognition or appreciation (on the part of both women and men) for the physical toll levied by these motherhood activities. For example, breastfeeding requires an additional 500 calories per day and an extra 20 grams of protein to maintain energy.

On an intellectual basis, most of us "know" these three wondrous stages of motherhood place real added demands on our physical bodies. And yet I've talked to countless pregnant, new and/or nursing mothers who exclaim in frustration, "I don't know why I feel so worn out."

Well, I do. I've spent all but fifteen months over the past eleven years pregnant and/or nursing a baby. Yet I can't count the number of times I've said out loud, "I don't know why I feel so exhausted." We find it so easy to forget that the most natural activities of motherhood are inherently tiring.

I remember the prenatal appointment, while I was carrying our first child, when I looked at the doctor and said, "I am *so* tired and sleepy all the time. I don't understand it." The doctor responded, "Your body is doing a lot of work. Of course, you're tired. You need the extra sleep."

How many miles do you suppose the average mother has lugged the average child by the time that child is too big to be carried? I've never seen the answer documented. But I doubt those Sherpa guides who pack supplies for Himalayan climbing expeditions have much more experience in the hiking and hauling department than most mothers of young children. We spend years at a time with constantly squirming loads slung in infant carriers, on baby backpacks, or propped on hips.

There's an old story—I don't know if it's true or not—about the legendary early twentieth century athlete, Jim Thorpe. As the story goes, Thorpe was recruited for an experiment in which he was asked to get down on the floor next to a baby and do everything the child did for the day. The alleged result was that this superbly conditioned athlete gave up, winded, after a few short hours. If this didn't actually happen to Jim Thorpe, it certainly could have. Because any adult expected to mimic the perpetual motion of any young child for a day would undoubtedly need a longer afternoon nap than the youngster.

While mothers aren't required to match their children's movements every day, they are expected to keep up with them (often more than one at a time). Sometimes it's not enough just to keep up either—you need to be a jump or two ahead! And the strain this challenge places on a mother's body may be considerable.

Many mothers could echo the feelings of the mother of two preschoolers who said: "From the time I get up in the morning until I get them tucked in at night, my entire day is focused on the boys. It's often 9 o'clock in the evening before I have any time to myself, and by then I'm so exhausted I just want to go to bed and get some sleep."

Such feelings of exhaustion ought to be expected. Even injuries are not uncommon, as I can attest from my own experience. One time when Andrew was three and Matthew two, I took both boys to a local playground. As naptime approached I told the boys we needed to go home. I quickly draped my exhausted two-year-old over my shoulder for the trek to the car, but not before Andrew began pitching a tantrum over having to leave. I finally had to grab his arm tightly and practically drag him to the car—with him struggling against me all the way. My arm hurt for days before I finally went to an orthopedist who diagnosed an acute case of tendonitis.

Just a few months ago I ran and snatched up an angry three-year-old who was chasing his nine-year-old brother with a plastic wiffle ball bat. (He wanted to bat right then, and was *sure* it was time for his turn again!) In the process I wrenched my back seriously enough to warrant two chiropractic treatments.

And then there are all those physically taxing things we do with our kids just for fun. Hiking, camping, canoeing, horseback-riding, and more. Even the fun stuff can play a taxing role in what amounts to a very physically demanding, stressful job.

The result? Motherhood is a physical marathon measured more in years than in miles. And what adds to the challenge is that we're seldom allowed to set our own pace. Usually we have no choice but to run with the pack.

Constant Demands

We had a doctor friend on staff at a busy metropolitan hospital. Two weekends a month he was on call, meaning he had to be ready to work at a moment's notice, twenty-four hours a day. Another physician left the hospital, and our friend for a time was on call three weekends a month. "The pressure was incredible," he said. "I didn't know how long I could handle it."

We realize being on call is stressful, whatever the job—

doctor, firefighter, minister, plumber, whatever. But what about mothers? Most of us, whether we're working in or out of the home, are on-call mothers twenty-four hours a day, every weekend of the month—and every month of the year.

"I never knew it was so constant!" exclaimed one single, forty-five-year-old woman who'd just adopted a child. "I thought you played with kids and then put them down for naps and you were 'off duty.' Then you got them up, bathed them, fed them supper and let them play while you were 'off duty' again. Then you put them to bed, got ten hours of sleep yourself and were 'off duty.' I just never realized it was so constant. You're never really off duty!"

She's right. And as a single parent she's finding the demands even more constant because there is no one for her to turn to and say, "It's your turn this time."

While many men and women regularly bring work home from the job, there's at least a physical distance and difference between work and home. Home can be a haven away from the responsibilities of the job. Not so for mothers.

Oh, it's not that I can't or don't find time and places in my home to rest. But there is not a room in my house, not a chair I ever sit in, where I can't look around and see a dozen visual reminders of some responsibility I have as a mother. If it's not something I need to do immediately, it's something I ought to do, or maybe even something I want to do. There is no getting away from the job of motherhood.

I love family camping trips. It's fun experiencing the outdoors with my kids. But family vacations are not getaways from the responsibilities of motherhood either. A big part of the job always goes along for the ride.

So I can identify (I suspect most mothers can) with the mother of two who accosted me recently. "You're the mother of five," she said. "Don't you ever wish you could just quit for a day? I do. I don't want a divorce. I'd never want to give up my kids. But I do sometimes wish I had twenty-four hours when I wasn't a mother, when I wasn't a wife, when I could just be me. To do what I want."

Hers is a very understandable feeling in view of motherhood's constant, and therefore stressful, demands.

Repetitious Demands

As unpredictable as motherhood is, it's hard for me to think of it as monotonous. Yet there are repetitious elements of my work, and sometimes repetition can become monotonous. And as job stress studies have shown, monotony can increase feelings of stress.

One mother of a toddler said: "I suppose I need a creative outlet. But right now I'm just trying to stay sane while reading *Curious George* a half-dozen times a day. It's not that taking care of my baby doesn't allow for creativity—it does. And I find it as rewarding and challenging as any job I've ever had. It's just that sometimes the creative moments get buried under mountains of dishes and laundry."

It is the mundane, the routine household chores which need to be done again and again and again that I find among the most naggingly stressful tasks of motherhood. I can philosophically tell myself there is something noble in all work, that every pan I scrub, every sock I wash, dry, and (if I'm lucky) match, is a little labor of love for the ones I love.

But the continuous repetition of mundane household tasks makes me often feel like a friend who once said, "I can believe there's something special, something mystical about mothering my children. But I can't feel anything 'spiritual' about doing housework."

When repetition becomes monotony, it can add to any mother's stress.

Overwhelming Demands

A mother of four children ranging in age from four to sixteen said, "I've come to realize I don't have the energy level I need to give my children the time and attention they need *and* be the perfect housekeeper, the perfect cook, the perfect wife. I'd like to do it all, but I just can't do it."

Most mothers I've talked to can identify with the mother of two high schoolers and a kindergartner who said, "Every now and then I look at what needs to be done and I have this fleeting feeling that I can actually make it all work, but then something happens and I realize that's just a delusion."

One of the reasons to-do lists can be so frustrating to mothers is there's always more that needs to be, or ought to be done than can possibly be accomplished today, this week or this month.

Both the impossible number of demands and the nagging awareness of all those things we never quite get to, can make us feel overwhelmed. Repetition can add to the feeling; I always feel overwhelmed when I walk into a bedroom my children and I straightened yesterday, and realize it's a bigger mess now than it was then. But there's also another factor at work here.

In her encouraging book, *And Then I Had Kids*, Susan Alexander Yates gives this anecdote: "Late one summer afternoon, my husband, Johnny, arrived home from work to find me in a state of excitement. As I stood dripping with sweat, a big grin spread over my face when I exclaimed, 'Hi, honey, I mowed the lawn for you.' An astonished but pleased look crossed Johnny's face.

"'What's gotten into you?' he asked.

"I replied, 'I'm not sure, but I know I feel good because I have finally done something that lasts more than two days.'"

In contrast to a freshly mowed lawn that may not need more attention for a week or two, Yates goes on to say, "It is often difficult for moms of young children to accomplish anything that seems to last longer than a few hours. In a house with five small children, I found that clean kids were dirty quickly, a neat house lasted only through naptime, and dinner was a far cry from a gourmet meal. . . . Reading *Green Eggs and Ham* by Dr. Seuss for the fourth time, putting on tennis shoes again, or cleaning up the kitchen only to have it dirty five minutes later is more likely to produce frustration than fulfillment."

Seldom can a mother step back and admire a job well done, because it's never done. At least for long. And when there's no sense of completion, the job-stress studies say there's no relief from the stress.

Varied Demands

A few years ago I served on the program committee for the annual convention of the Chicago Association for the Education of Young Children, held at a big downtown hotel. Before a session in one of the hotel conference rooms, I realized the overhead projector wasn't set up yet. So I hurriedly unrolled the cord and began exploring the seminar room for the nearest electrical outlet. Just as I plugged it in, the hotel "electrician" walked up and chewed me out for doing his job. According to the hotel's union rules, he was the only one who was supposed to make electrical connections. I thought his reaction was a little absurd (though not as absurd as his bill for "electrical services"), because, like most mothers, I'm used to doing whatever needs doing whenever it needs to be done.

Homes are not union shops where we have to worry about stepping on toes if we accidentally do someone else's job. In fact, a mother's job description is as broad as it is long. In an age of growing specialization, motherhood still demands a jill-of-all-trades.

Thinking about the diversity of my job one day this week, I sat down at lunchtime and made a list of everything I remembered doing that morning. My accomplishments ranged from calling a repair man to fix our refrigerator, to playing referee to ten children in our yard, to learning by trial and error to French-braid my daughter's hair, to typing part of this book on my computer. And of course, I prepared breakfast and lunch, washed those dishes, did three loads of laundry, changed diapers, and nursed a baby.

It wasn't an unusual morning at all. Routinely I have to shift gears so quickly and so often I probably ought to drive myself to AAMCO every few months for a personal transmission check. Shifting gears from one role to another is just part of any mother's job.

Think about it. On any given day a mother could be expected to be a nurse, teacher, cook, maid, purchasing agent, coach, mediator, mechanic, tailor, fashion consultant, chauffeur, gardener, entertainer, accountant, dispatcher, secretary, counselor, delivery person, business manager, and much more. Many of these roles are handled simultaneously.

But it sometimes feels impossible to integrate such diverse demands. I say this as I try to write at an old Kaypro computer propped on a small desk crammed in my laundry room. Even as the keyboard clicks beneath my fingers, the overall buckles clack noisily in the dryer right behind me.

The first frustration resulting from such varied demands is a lack of focus. A mother's mind is constantly pulled in a hundred or so different directions at the same time. Seldom can we concentrate exclusively on one of our major roles as a mother, let alone on a single task. How many different things do we try to accomplish while we're getting supper on the table at night?

A related question: How many interruptions do we have in the course of preparing a simple supper?

"In the list of things that get to me," said one mother of four, "I'd have to put 'interruptions' near the top. Just when you think you have a block of time to do something, the interruptions start. And it's not just the little 'Mommy-can-I-have-a-drink?' interruptions. Often it's something significant that has to be done immediately."

Interruptions are frequently tied to the big issues of unpredictability and lack of control, but they are also a natural outgrowth of a job with so many constantly changing and varied demands. The result being that many mothers rarely experience the simple, satisfying peace to be found in single-minded concentration on a task or problem. And this inability to focus is both frustrating and stressful.

*   *   *

A mother's job is demanding. The nature of the work requires both the managerial skills of a corporate executive and the sweat of a day-laborer. The demands are at once physically exhausting, unrelentingly constant, monotonously repetitious, often overwhelmingly and incredibly varied.

It all adds up to hard, stressful work.

7

Modern-day Motherhood Stresses

My Grandmother Shaw's life as a mother must have been a hard one in many ways. She raised five active sons in a rural Georgia mill town. Her husband, my grandfather, labored in the textile mill ten to twelve hours a day and then worked as a barber after supper most nights and weekends.

Yet, in many ways, when I am feeling overwhelmed by the daily details of housework, I envy Mama Shaw. She kept her house so clean, my father reported, that one could safely eat off her floors. I can only wonder, *How did she do it?*

Her granddaughter's floors are too seldom mopped and constantly cluttered. Even with all my wonderful modern conveniences, I fight a full-pitched battle just to keep my family from getting lost beneath great heaps of laundry and dirty dishes. I live with cobwebs, dusty furniture, and windows with a bigger collection of fingerprints than the FBI archives. Floors clean enough to eat off of? Forget it. I'd be happy if my floors were just clean enough to walk on—without stumbling over some toy!

When my grandmother raised her family, she didn't have the household technology I have to help with the basic household tasks of cooking, cleaning, and laundry. But I've recently come to recognize she also didn't have some of the additional demands that fall to me as a mother today.

In her later years, Mama Shaw's grocery shopping was done

by handing a detailed grocery list to my grandfather. He went to the store and brought the groceries home for her. When her children were young, she, like many mothers of her day, had the store deliver the groceries.

Mama Shaw didn't spend hours every week chauffeuring her children to school, music lessons or t-ball games. In fact, she never owned a driver's license. Why should she? She was never expected to drive anywhere. Her sons didn't consider it her responsibility to transport them anywhere; they walked or hitched rides wherever they wanted to go.

My grandparents were working class people, yet my grandmother hired a laundress to wash her family's clothes. Only the very poorest townspeople of her era did their own laundry. And her laundress helped with the cleaning and cooking as well.

My grandmother did not spend time reading up on child-rearing—she followed the example and advice of her mother and grandmother who lived nearby. She didn't thumb through women's magazines in search of interesting new dinners to enchant her husband or her friends. She fixed simple, wholesome meals with what foods were in season and could be afforded. She didn't have a dozen cookbooks which took up space and needed to be dusted either!

When her children were young, Mama Shaw spent no time purchasing, using, cleaning, or arranging to repair a blender, food processor, microwave oven, dishwasher, crockpot, electric can-opener, television, VCR, washer, dryer, freezer, toaster, or any number of other conveniences common today. She was not responsible for seeing that the oil was changed in the family car (I am) or that it was taken in for a tune-up (again usually my job).

Nor did she spend several hours each month balancing the checkbook and writing checks to pay bills (one of my jobs). And if one of her sons became sick, she didn't go to the doctor's office and spend an hour waiting, and another thirty minutes in the examination room, then yet another hour getting a prescription filled at the pharmacy. She dosed her sick children with a home remedy or some medicine my grandfather picked up at the store. If one became sicker, the doctor came by to look at the child. She did not take her sons to see the dentist every six months, or help them floss their teeth each night.

She didn't take Trouble, the family bulldog, to the veterinarian, either. (Although, since Trouble was aptly named, she probably spent as much time bandaging his wounds from dog fights as I do taking our dog to the vet for routine checkups and shots.)

Mama Shaw has a handful of precious photographs of her children and family, carefully protected in a few albums. She loved photographs and collected more than many women of her generation. But I have boxes full of prints in our basement, waiting until I can afford the money and time to buy photo albums to get them all organized. After that, I'll need to find the time to arrange all our slides in carousels. And I really want to get our 8 mm movies of my oldest children as babies converted to videotape.

I don't mean to say Mama Shaw's life was easy compared to mine. She raised her five sons in the days when each meal was cooked from scratch in hard-to-clean pots and eaten from plates that had to be washed by hand. I, on the other hand, frequently use paper plates, and whenever I use dishes, can put them, unrinsed, into a dishwasher.

But where I once thought my life as a mother—with dishwashers and many other modern conveniences—should be much easier than Mama Shaw's, I now realize it is merely difficult in different ways. Where our modern technology and culture has indeed made some parts of motherhood easier, there are many other modern day stressors our grandmothers, and in some cases even our mothers, never faced.

We'll look at a sampling of these modern-day stresses in this chapter and the next:

The Housework Hustle

As we plunge into the twenty-first century with the construction industry talking about the computer-controlled homes of tomorrow, we're reminded just how far household technology has progressed in the past 100 years. Long gone are the days of cooking with wood fires, scrubbing floors with homemade lye soap, and laundering clothes by hand with washboards in tubs of water drawn by the bucketful from a well or spring. Most mothers today find it nearly impossible to imagine how our grandmothers and great-grandmothers coped in the days before self-cleaning ovens, vacuum cleaners, and permanent press clothing. At least housework is simpler, faster, and less stressful today. Right?

Not necessarily, according to Ruth Schwartz Cowan in her book *More Work for Mother*, which is subtitled *The Ironies of Household Technology from the Open Hearth to the Microwave*. Her in-depth survey of housework since the 1600s brought her to some very interesting conclusions. She convincingly contends that the vast majority of cultural changes and technological improvements in all three major areas of housework—cooking, cleaning and laundry—have had two results. They have either (1) raised expectations and standards to a level unimaginable to women of previous generations, or (2) shifted responsibilities from others and onto mothers. The bottom line, as Cowan claims in her book's title, is *more* work for mothers, not less.

Consider laundry as an example. Sure, it's easier to wash clothes in today's machines with push-button wash-and-rinse controls than it was to use a corrugated metal washboard and squeeze the rinse water out by hand. And my washer's a big improvement over my grandmother's first wringer washer. But the end result of all the laundry "improvements" is a higher standard of cleanliness for our clothes. Where our grandmothers had one "laundry day" a week (when they did three or four tubfuls of clothes), I do at least a couple of loads almost every day and ten to fifteen loads every week. Where our grandmothers would brush dried mud off overalls to make them "wearable" for another few days, if my daughter dribbles milk on her blouse during breakfast, I toss it into the dirty clothes and find her a clean top to wear to school. So, while washing a load of clothes is certainly easier today than it used to be, mothers today wash many more clothes, much more often. And that mountain of laundry must all be sorted, folded, and put away. We may actually spend more time on laundry than our grandmothers did.

In the days before vacuum cleaners, carpets (if a house had them) were carried out and beaten a couple times a year. And even if beating rugs was sometimes a woman's job, hauling the carpet out was almost always man's work. Today, vacuuming is a weekly and sometimes daily task, done, in the vast majority of cases, by women.

And while the modern convenience of running water has revolutionized cooking and sanitary practices, it too has shifted a bigger share of the load onto women. Where men and children often hauled buckets of water from wells for cooking and bathing, today the tasks of cleaning kitchen sinks and scrubbing bathrooms (as well as calling the plumber) tend to fall to women.

Cooking has seen a similar trend. Where men hunted and helped raise the food for the family table in the past, women today purchase most food. And at the same time kitchen appliances, frozen foods and instant mixes have made meal preparation "simple," the recipes we attempt are more complicated and the food we serve is more varied than anything our grandmothers imagined.

According to historian Cowan, most advances in household technology came as the result of industrialization—as more and more nineteenth and early twentieth century men left home and farm to work in towns and factories, women needed all the technological help they could get as they assumed responsibility for more and more areas of household management which had always been shared. But, says Cowan, "The modern technological systems on which our households and our standard of living depend were constructed on the assumption that women would remain at home, that they would continue to function as pre-industrial workers (without pay, time clocks, or supervisors) . . . and not enter the labor market except under unusual (and usually temporary) circumstances."

However, today the majority of mothers work outside the home. And the shift of added household responsibility to women, combined with today's higher standards in all areas of housework, has resulted in very little total timesaving at home.

This "progress" has taken a big toll according to Cowan, "a toll measured in the hours that employed housewives have to work in order to perform adequately first as employees and then as housewives. A 35-hour week (housework) added to a 40-hour week (paid employment) adds up to a working week that even sweatshops cannot match."

So whether or not a mother is employed outside the home, however many "conveniences" she has in her home, housework is still time-consuming, stressful work. Just as it was for our grandmothers and their grandmothers.

Mobility

Some modern stresses we face today are very different from our grandmothers' experiences. My Mama Shaw still lives in the same house she's lived in for more than fifty years—in the same town she's lived in for almost seventy-five years. My husband's Grandma Lewis was born in a Michigan log cabin, moved half a mile down the road to get married, and lived in that farmhouse until she died some sixty years later.

In contrast, I've lived in seven different homes (apartments and houses) in three different states during my sixteen years of marriage. I recently read that the average American moves four-teen times. Many women today have moved a lot more. (In fact, one mother I talked to, whose husband was a professional base-ball player, had moved a staggering *thirty-two times* in eight years of marriage.) But my last move, over seven hundred miles, with four kids and a dog, when I was six-months pregnant, reminded me how stressful moving can be.

Everyone recognizes the stress of changing jobs. But when a husband or a wife walks into a new place of employment there are usually many familiar elements to the new job. And however drastic the change, "work" is still only about a third of the day.

When you move to a new home, the family's entire life changes. And it's usually the mother who faces the brunt of that change. Every home is different and requires adjustments in chores and management of the household. Both before and after a move, thousands of decisions, big and little, have to be made about what goes where and who does what. Family routines have to be adjusted, sometimes drastically.

It's usually the mother who has to learn how to meet most of her family's needs in a new community. What stores have the best buys on what products? What grocery store has the best produce? The biggest selection of generic products? Where's the cheapest place to buy milk? What doctors are available and what are their reputations? How about veterinarians? What do you have to know about the new schools? New churches? Who do you call to repair your air conditioner? What newspaper should you subscribe to?

Every time you move, a million such questions require answers. Daily routines are disrupted and must be completely reconstructed. And the stressful implications of that myriad of changes goes on for months before and, according to one expert I read, approximately eighteen months *after* every move.

So modern day mobility definitely adds to motherhood stress.

Choices, Choices

When Mama Shaw sent my grandfather to the store for groceries, she didn't have to compare this week's sale prices on hamburger to know where to send him. There was one little grocer in town who carried staples and a narrow selection of other items. If that store didn't have something, Mama Shaw went without. In contrast, the town of 30,000 where I live has eight large supermarkets representing five major chains. And I couldn't begin to guess the number of convenience stores which probably carry as many products as Mama Shaw's small-town grocer did in the 1920s.

Just twenty years ago, when the best-seller *Future Shock* popularized the concept of "overchoice," not even a man as imaginative and prophetic as author Alvin Toffler could have dreamed of the selection of products now available in any one of the chain supermarkets in my town. A recent *Los Angeles Times* article on consumer choice began by asking, "Have you visited your local

Cereal Aisle from Hell lately?" Some stores stock more than forty varieties of oat bran cereal alone.

Quoting the *Los Angeles Times*, "You say you're getting a headache from just thinking about cereal choices? The health-aids aisle could conceivably make things worse. Even if you've figured out the difference between aspirin, acetaminophen and ibuprofen (and you know whether you want regular or extra strength formulas—with or without sinus, arthritis or antacid medication thrown in), you then face the capsules-tablets-or-caplets decision."

Even the old classics now require a choice. Spam comes in four varieties, including Spam Lite.

Jeremy Rifkin, president of the Washington-based Foundation of Economic Trends, says, "You can go into a major shopping mall and become totally emotionally exhausted in one hour, and you might have been in only one store buying one item. The reason is that there is such a plethora of items to pick from and so much stimuli in front of you that people have a hard time focusing . . . . People are really emotionally stressed—and don't know it—from the tremendous proliferation of consumer items and the terrific assessments they have to make when they buy a product."

Rifkin points out that shoppers are asked to simultaneously weigh a product's environmental impact, its implication for health and safety, and even social responsibility questions such as what country it's produced in and whether or not the manufacturer is a fair and responsible employer. The result of all this, according to Rifkin, is "a tremendous emotional burden well beyond the level [of stress] that our parents knew 20 years ago."

While the problem of overchoice is probably most obvious in consumer goods, it occurs in almost every area of our lives. Where my Mama Shaw used the services of the town doctor, my recent move to a new town meant I had to select from scores of doctors listed in the yellow pages. And while my grandmother sent her boys to school and church and expected them to find their own creative outlets among the fields, forests and rivers in their home community, my children and their friends also have the option of Boy Scouts, Girl Scouts, Cub Scouts, Brownies, organized sports (t-ball, baseball, soccer, football, basketball, track, tennis, and swimming—provided by schools, the county recreation department, the YMCA and sometimes churches), park district classes in dance, art, or exercise. There are music and theatre programs, and much more. All this requires decision-making, time and energy—and adds stress to motherhood.

Much of the choice overload mothers face today regards more pressing questions than "What kind of frozen vegetables will I serve my family for supper?" or "What summer program will I sign my kids up for down at the park?" We have major life choices never afforded earlier generations.

Many families today can even choose what part of the country they live in. We have more choice than any other generation in history about how many children we'll have—and when we'll have them.

Then there's the choice of birth control itself—complete with its moral, health, and sexual implications.

And what about all the choices possible in child-rearing, starting with a mother's decisions about childbirth? Natural or medicated? Hospital or home? Then breast-fed or bottles? What strategy will you choose for discipline? Walk into any bookstore and just count the titles offering "fresh, new" advice on how best to bring up your children.

The most crucial and the most insignificant areas of our modern lives offer a multitude of stressful choices that *must* be made. And a large percentage of those choices are made by mothers.

* * *

So many women I've talked to judge their own performance against the standards set by their mothers and grandmothers. They figure the advantages afforded by modern motherhood must make mothering easier today. They think, *If my mother and grandmother did it, why am I so stressed?* and feel all the more inadequate.

The truth is, we face most of the age-old stresses of motherhood—and a lot of new ones our mother and grandmothers never had to deal with. We'll look at a few more of these modern stressors in the next chapter.

8

More Modern-day Motherhood Stresses

There are still more stresses I face that my Grandmother Shaw didn't have to deal with when she became a mother seventy years ago.

Current and Future Fears

I sat with a small group of mothers recently as we honestly confessed some of the personal fears we have for our children. A mother of three young children voiced the concerns of millions of mothers the world over when she said, "I can't help worrying about the threat of nuclear war in my children's lifetime."

"You read and hear so much about the dangers of pesticides in our food. I can't even encourage my kids to eat something healthy like apples without worrying if I'm doing more harm than good," complained another mom.

Other environmental fears mentioned included the disappearing ozone, chemical pollution, the world food shortage, and the growing threat of nuclear waste. "I worry about the kind of world my children are inheriting," one young mother said, "and I feel so powerless to do anything to protect them." (Lack of control again.)

Even without considering the future, there's enough to worry about today. As one mother said, "You can't even feel safe sending your kids to school—what with all the drugs and violence today." Everyone in the group thought about the headline stories a few weeks earlier when a disturbed young man fired an automatic assault rifle into a crowded California schoolyard, killing five children and wounding many more. And I thought of a school teacher I know who lives within fifty miles of me in north Georgia; she told me about a recent safety training program at her school where all the county elementary teachers were instructed in how to react if an armed intruder walked into their classrooms—including what to do if he opened fire on the children.

Then there's the threat of kidnapping and the even greater incidences of sexual abuse and molestation of children, and many other potential worries.

In one recent survey of its readers conducted by the *Ladies' Home Journal*, mothers were asked, "What worries you most about raising your children?" Forty-three percent of the women responding said they worried about "protecting children from drug use." Thirty-six percent were worried about "the media and peers undercutting parental authority." Twenty-nine percent worried about working and not being home full-time, while twenty percent worried about economic instability in their children's future. And seventeen percent worried about protecting children from AIDS.

It's not as if we mothers today spend every waking hour in a state of perpetual anxiety over the safety and security of our children's lives. But we wouldn't be realistic if we didn't recognize many valid reasons to worry about the welfare of the babies we brought into this dangerous, fallen world.

Fear is stressful. And most of the modern fears my friends and I discussed in that group are new in our generation.

Again, let me say I'm not trying to belittle the real fears felt by earlier generations of mothers. My Mama Shaw worried about her boys' health whenever a new epidemic of childhood disease swept through the community. She feared for their safety every time they risked the forbidden by skinny-dipping in the swift muddy waters of the Yellow River. But I don't think she ever felt the futile sense of helplessness and the nagging fear I live with in a world where a mother can't feed her children fresh fruit or send them to school without weighing the risks.

There's no way to measure the effect of living with such fears. But common sense and everything we know about human psychology today tells us our modern-day worries have to add to our modern-day stress.

Today's Family Infrastructure

Mobility, which itself increases motherhood stress in the variety of ways we've already discussed, contributes to another significant modern stress—the fragmented family. As we routinely move hundreds of miles away from extended families, we have destroyed the most significant motherhood support system—the traditional natural network of relatives who have always been a new mother's best hope for stress-relief in the form of emotional reassurance, parenthood training, and child-care assistance.

This deemphasis on the extended family has also contributed to another of the stresses discussed earlier in the book—inadequate preparation for motherhood. Women of our grandmothers' generation had ample opportunity to observe and care for younger siblings or the babies of older siblings, of aunts, or of cousins. Today, many, if not most, mothers in western culture have never even held a three-day-old newborn until they come home from the hospital with full and complete responsibility for their own child.

Today's fragmented families create other very different stresses on motherhood. The proliferation of divorce and the growing incidence of blended families resulting from remarriage make for tremendous stress on any mother who experiences either. A complicated task becomes all the more complex.

"Motherhood was tough enough before," said one recently remarried mother of two. "Now I'm learning to be a wife to my new husband and stepmother to his children. And I'm having to help my children build a positive relationship with their new stepfather and his family. And my ex-husband and his family are critical of my new husband to the children. The tension when the children come home from visiting their father is unbelievable!"

And then there are single mothers. One of them said, "Just being a mother is hard, stressful work. Trying to be both a mother and a father to my kids is worse. Most days it's impossible."

The deterioration of the family today—both extended and nuclear—has increased motherhood stress.

Changing Roles

As women's roles have drastically changed over the last couple of generations a chasm has formed—one that effectively separates women into two distinct camps: those who choose to stay home and those employed outside the home. Whichever camp we belong to, there's an unnatural, undeniable barrier which denies us that traditional supportive sense of mutual understanding and shared experience with the other "half" of the female population. Mothers in each group wrestle with the realization that they're missing out on something millions of other mothers experience. And the resulting tension naturally adds to modern motherhood's stress.

But the changing roles of women in contemporary society don't just affect their relationships with other women. As the sex-role boundaries separating masculine and feminine have shifted, many husbands and wives have been left unsure of where they stand. It's no longer as simple as saying, "My mother did this and my father did that, so I'll do this and you do that."

Lack of role definition creates stress in any job. And it opens the door for potential abuse if one party shifts too much of the load onto the other.

One mother of two children, then aged two and three, told about her marriage: "As far as Tom was concerned, his job was to go to work, bring home his paycheck, and fish and relax. Since all I had to do was watch two children, keep house, cook meals, and do laundry, surely I could fill *all* my free time with doing the bills, mowing the lawn, and anything else that he thought needed to be done. And, of course, since I didn't work, I could get up when the children were sick in the night.

"Then, whenever our money was tight, he would bug me to go back to work. He'd ask how I could stand to stay at home and 'not do anything.'

"Now that we are divorced, on the weekends when the children are with him, he stays at his mother's house. That way he still doesn't have to do any of the work of parenting. His mother does it. And he still believes that I 'didn't work' while we were married!"

Obviously, few marriages are this extreme, but, in far too many cases, there is the unspoken assumption that a mother's workload is lighter and that she, therefore, can handle a bigger share of family responsibilities and tasks.

Whatever procedure we use today to work out the sex roles in our marital relationships—and even if we come to a mutually satisfactory agreement—the process itself takes time, effort, and clear communication. And that automatically adds stress.

Media Messages

Most of us are so conditioned to seeing television (and the rest of the electronic media) in terms of entertainment and relaxation that we seldom recognize its power as a cultural force. We don't often think about what it teaches us or how it's made our lives different from those of pre-TV generations.

Unfortunately, what television says to and about mothers usually adds to motherhood stress. Problem number one is the unrealistic model of motherhood pictured by television. To start with, most women on TV, especially the most interesting and glamorous women, are not portrayed as mothers at all. Those who are, live in immaculate houses free of realistic clutter and seldom ever engage in those unglamorous, time-consuming tasks that make up so much of a mother's job. To distort the picture even further, the most serious problems faced by television mothers are always resolved by the end of a thirty- or sixty-minute episode.

When you consider the image of mothers and motherhood portrayed on TV, and then realize that study after study has shown how television shapes many viewers' perception of reality, a serious problem becomes obvious. When we compare, consciously or unconsciously, the reality of our own motherhood with the false reality we see on TV, the disconcerting difference can add dissatisfaction and stress. And if, as some communication experts insist, what we see on TV validates our experience, most of what we do as mothers is thereby judged invalid and insignificant.

And then there are television commercials, many of which try to sell products by creating false stress. The unspoken accusation is that we can't be good mothers unless we serve our families a particular kind of soup, get rid of the yellow waxy buildup on our kitchen floors, and can see our reflections in our everyday china. We should be able to "bring home the bacon, fry it up in a pan, and never, never let him forget he's a man." Such advertisers not only attempt to create a stress their product can then relieve, but they perpetuate a myth of meaninglessness that says, in effect, women in general—and mothers in particular—don't have any more serious concerns.

Modern Medicine

Despite all the good modern medicine does and has done—the routine wizardry regularly performed in operating rooms, the wonders of "miracle cures" which have brought an end to so many diseases that threatened the world for generations—our medical establishment has created its own modern stresses on motherhood, especially in the areas of pregnancy and childbirth.

Sheila Kitzinger, a noted British social anthropologist and childbirth educator who has studied motherhood in cultures around the world, points out this problem with modern childbirth in her book, *Women as Mothers*:

"Many mothers are persuaded that only if every technique

and every available machine is used are they giving babies the best chance, and fathers are often even more readily convinced. One consequence is the failure of confidence in handling and relating to the infant, a basic lack of trust in the ability to mother one's own baby. This is such a familiar syndrome in the West that we hardly comment on it any more, anticipating that the new mother will be awkward, unsure of herself, anxious and readily distressed. But this particular psychological reaction to motherhood is almost unknown in peasant cultures, where birth takes place at home and where the new mother cares for her baby from the moment of delivery with the help of other women members of her own or her husband's family."

From obstetricians who "take charge" of a woman's pregnancy, to the maternity nurses who whisk a newborn baby out of a mother's arms at the slightest provocation or whim of hospital schedules, to the pediatrician who tells her what, how, and when to feed her baby, the message modern medicine gives mothers is, "We know your job better than you do." In so doing, modern medicine certainly contributes to, and may even create, the deep stressful feelings of inadequacy felt by so many young mothers today.

While it's true, as we've admitted, that many modern mothers are woefully unprepared for the reality and responsibility of motherhood (for lack of training and other reasons), there must be a better solution to this problem than abdicating primary responsibility for the natural, God-designed passage into motherhood to the increasingly unnatural, impersonal, often humiliating procedures of "modern" childbirth.

In medicine's well-meaning attempt to reduce the natural risks (and stress) surrounding childbirth, it's produced a medical technology that creates new risks of its own. It then must counter this with new technology and new risks. And not even the "natural childbirth" movement of the past two decades has stopped the trend.

Certainly some mothers today owe the lives of their children to the miracle of modern medical technology. We needn't be antimedicine. But neither should we discount the value of our

God-given instincts as women and mothers. Kitzinger writes, "Given a 'facilitating environment,' that is, one that gives the parents themselves emotional support and allows them to develop confidence, most parents spontaneously enjoy their new babies, for example, and handle and talk to them in a manner which is tuned and synchronized in just the right way to the baby's needs and the non-verbal signal which it is sending out. The sad thing is that our own maternity hospitals rarely provide such a facilitating environment."

By not fully respecting or affirming a woman's own role in those very first critical stages of motherhood, modern medicine creates for us (and created for our mothers) a modern stress our grandmothers and great-grandmothers never knew.

Who Can We Trust?

Sociologists don't all agree on its origin—perhaps it began with the sudden, sobering end of "Camelot" when President John F. Kennedy was assassinated; the roots may lie in the national disillusionment that resulted from America's wrenching Vietnam experience; it could be a byproduct of a personal impotence fostered by the threat of nuclear annihilation; or maybe there are other reasons. Whatever the causes, most observers of modern culture would agree there's a crisis of trust in the institutions of our world. But what we mothers today often see as healthy skepticism of authorities—and especially the resulting drive to assume more personal responsibility for every area of our lives—naturally results in new, added stress.

The multiplying numbers of health-oriented books and magazines, as well as all the available volumes of laymen's medical reference books, are a good example.

I have read enough to know how little many doctors know about the side effects or the potentially harmful interactions of the drug combinations they prescribe. I also realize that drug companies themselves are the primary source of information doctors get about drugs. Thus I, like a number of my mother-friends, keep a copy of a current consumer-reference book, _The People's_

Pharmacy, on a family reference bookshelf in my home. And having several times been given or had prescribed dangerous (in a couple of cases potentially lethal) combinations of drugs by doctors and other health-care authorities, I wouldn't think of taking or dispensing any medication to my family without first finding out just what that medicine is, what it does, and what it's not supposed to do.

In a sense, the knowledge available in popular reference books today can relieve some of the stress we feel, some of the healthy distrust we have for modern health-care. For example, Dr. Robert Mendelsohn's eye-opening book, *How to Raise a Healthy Child in Spite of Your Doctor,* has relieved some of my own motherhood stress by encouraging and enabling me to confidently make more medical decisions for myself and my family. But at the same time, the disconcerting information I learn in the course of my personal medical education, and the added responsibility I feel for assuring and protecting the health of my family makes it impossible for me to trust today's medical establishment in the same way my grandmother trusted the small town family doctor who provided medical services to her family. And that means a new, modern stress for me.

A similar distrust of authority occurs today regarding educational institutions. Where many of our grandparents had the simple rule: *A whipping at school deserves another whipping at home,* few parents today hold the same blind trust in a school's or a teacher's judgment. Many mothers today see and feel the necessity for fully understanding not only any reasons for discipline, but experience similar concerns for every aspect of our children's educational experiences—from the curriculum our children are taught to the teaching style employed by their teachers.

I talked with one mother of two grade-schoolers who experienced severe motherhood stress when the public school, and particularly her gifted son's teacher, were unable to challenge the first-grader and seemed oblivious to the boy's special needs. This mother told me: "My husband's mother can't understand my concern at all. She sent the kids off every morning and didn't give it a second thought. She saw no reason to be concerned about what was going on at school. She simply trusted the school and the teachers.

"But I agonize over what happens to my kids at school. And while I have more trust in the school we've transferred the kids to, I still don't feel the people there are infallible. I don't feel they always know exactly what is best for every single child. So I want and need to know what's going on."

While parent involvement in schools is needed—and is encouraged by most good educators today—that involvement means new responsibility. And that, too, adds stress.

We don't, either as a society or as individuals, have as much faith in the institution of government our grandparents had—which isn't too surprising after Watergate and countless scandals since. The institution of religion doesn't always inspire trust either—also not surprising at the close of a century during which a sizeable school of noted theologians declared "God is dead," and at the end of a decade in which the well-publicized behavior of some of his most visible proponents would have been enough to set even a deceased deity spinning in his grave.

If one effect of our lack of trust in institutions is that it forces us to take more individual responsibility and make more informed, personal decisions regarding everything in our lives from our health to our faith, then much of our skepticism is healthy. But whether our lack of trust in our society's basic institutions is good or bad, it's certainly yet another modern source of stress.

*   *   *

These are a few of the modern-day stresses I've felt personally or that have been expressed by the mothers I've known and interviewed. You may have felt many others.

But the bottom line is this: On top of all the reasons for stress mothers have traditionally known, we have some big new ones our grandmothers never encountered.

9

Hidden Stressors

Early one summer morning after my husband had gone to work, I herded four small children into the car and set out on a twenty-five minute drive to my sister's house in another Chicago suburb. My parents, who lived out of state, had been visiting Illinois for a few days and I wanted to see them one more time before they headed home later in the day.

The morning rush hour had already peaked; traffic on the familiar route was only moderate. My four squirmy children obviously weren't too excited about being confined in a car, even for a few minutes, on such a beautiful sunshiny morning. Fourteen-month-old Benjamin, who was teething at the time, fussed constantly in his carseat beside me.

While we waited at a traffic light halfway to my sister's, I handed Benjamin a toy I thought might distract him for a time, patted his leg, and tried to sweet-talk him into a happier mood. It seemed to help.

The light turned green and the car in front of me began to move. I returned my attention to the road and moved my foot from the brake to the gas pedal. Just as the car began to accelerate, Benjamin screamed. I instinctively glanced over at him, for only a split second. When I looked up again, the driver in front of me had hit his brakes. I stomped on mine, but too late. My big station wagon skidded into the rear end of a compact import car.

Fortunately, no one was hurt. But the low-speed impact resulted in $700 damage to our car and more to the car I'd hit. After a policeman filled out the accident report and issued me a "failure-to-stop" citation, I drove on to my sister's, feeling very grateful the accident had been no worse, and experiencing incredible stress.

Hidden Stressor #1: Driving

I don't know that I'd consciously thought about driving being a motherhood stress until a few years ago when I read a magazine article entitled "Tending Children at 50 Miles Per Hour." The title stuck with me. What mother doesn't know what it's like to divide her attention between the crying baby beside her and the traffic flow ahead? Between a petty quarrel in the back seat and the semi with his blinker on in the next lane?

So when you consider what safety experts say—that the leading cause of automobile accidents (apart from alcohol) is doing something else while driving—you see that driving provides a very real, if sometimes overlooked, stress (and danger!) for us mothers. Incongruity creates stress. And what could be more incongruous than the conflict that often arises when we drive, that conflict between highway safety (which we all know demands our fullest attention at all times) and a mother's instinctive response to a child's need?

You don't even have to be driving fifty miles per hour. Ten or fifteen was too fast the morning of my accident.

And whether she enjoys sitting behind the wheel or not, anyone who spends hours a week on the road has to admit driving itself often creates a certain level of stress. We're not talking joy rides or scenic pleasure driving here.

As one mother said, "Some weeks I feel more a chauffeur, or a taxi driver than a mother. I drop kids off at three different schools every morning before I go to work. Which means three different stops every afternoon, too. That doesn't include scout meetings, ball games, piano lessons, our children's choir practice at church, or kids' visits to friends' homes." Without any help from a central dispatcher telling her where to go next, mom is responsible for knowing all destinations. And, unlike professional taxi drivers, she's fully responsible for delivering her passengers, not only on time, but suitably attired and emotionally prepared for whatever is to happen next.

And then there are the little worries that go along with chauffeuring children. I used to wonder what I would do if I had car trouble with four small children in the car (I knew I couldn't very well walk for help). But I also remembered the time (before I had children) when I sat for an hour with the hood of my car up, on the shoulder of a Chicago expressway, and watched three different police cars whiz by without even slowing down before I finally climbed a fence and hiked to a gas station in a strange neighborhood of the city. What would I have done if I'd had kids with me? The question was always there, at least in the far recesses of my mind, every time I backed out of our suburban Chicago driveway.

Today, living in the rural mountains of northern Georgia, I still wonder. Traffic is often sparse and the houses are few and far between on some of the roads I now travel regularly with five children—the youngest only a few months old. What would I do if I got stranded?

One mother told me about the time she and her husband were driving down the highway with their two toddlers when their car's engine caught fire. They skidded to a halt on the side of the road. The mother pulled her fifteen-month-old daughter out of her car seat and the father yanked their two-and-a-half-year-old boy out of his without even unbuckling the safety harness. Then both parents ran for safety, away from the burning vehicle. No one was hurt. But that mother had nightmares for weeks.

"I kept wondering what I would have done if I'd been alone," she said. "I couldn't gave gotten both children out of that burning car at once. What if I'd had to choose which of my children to save first?"

The "what if" questions can add to the ordinary stress of driving to make it one of the biggest, most common hidden stressors for many mothers. Yet driving is only one of many hidden stresses in motherhood. We'll discuss a number of others in this chapter and the next.

I'd like to start by telling you how I discovered the most bothersome, most insidious hidden stress I personally feel as a mother.

Hidden Stressor #2: Noise

Somewhere along about the time my third baby was born I began worrying about my hearing. My husband and I would be sitting in the family room and Gregg would ask, "Want me to check on Lisette? It sounds like she's awake."

I'd listen for noise from the other end of the house: "I didn't hear anything."

A few moments later Gregg would say, "I think she's fussing." I'd heard nothing. But sure enough, one of us would check and find a tearful baby.

My father had experienced a severe loss of hearing after the age of sixty. Hearing loss is a hereditary problem in my family. But I wasn't ready to be losing mine in my thirties!

I found it troubling to have to ask Gregg to turn up the volume so I could understand the dialog on a TV program. I hated to ask one of the children to repeat a whispered question or comment. I often felt a dull ache in my ears and sometimes the sharp pains of a tight headache seemed to center in the area behind my ears.

Could I really be losing my hearing? I made an appointment with an ear, nose and throat specialist. He gave me a thorough exam and ran some auditory tests before telling me my hearing tested normal and he could find nothing wrong. When I said I thought I suffered a real reduction in my hearing in the presence of a combination of background noises, he shrugged and said everyone did—some people more than others probably, but he had no way of testing that sort of discriminatory hearing.

I went home relieved to know this ENT specialist didn't think deafness was imminent for me. But I was frustrated not to have some explanation as to why my ears continued to bother me.

Months later, in a very interesting book, *The Female Stress Syndrome* by Dr. Georgia Witkin-Lanoil, I read her brief discussion of what she called "noise stress." She listed a couple of dozen daily noises from any mother's world and said noise stress was often intensified because mothers develop a special knack for listening for noises—most of which signify some sort of responsibility.

Just reading the term "noise stress" triggered a chain reaction of thoughts in my mind. It was one of life's great "aha!" experiences for me.

I closed the book, got a notebook and pen, sat down at my kitchen table and began my own list of the noises of my world as a mother—noises that not only might be stressful in and of themselves, but noises that also signified responsibility and the stress that goes with it. I filled the page, two columns wide, and turned to the back without even slowing down. I finally quit writing, not because I ran out of things I could list, but because of writer's cramp.

As I paused to look over what I'd written I thought, *No wonder my ears bother me! Look at all the noises they're subjected to! Look at all the things they have to listen for!*

Rereading that list I'd scribbled down as fast as I could think in four or five short minutes was an incredibly comforting revelation for me. I wasn't experiencing permanent hearing loss! I was experiencing a very understandable case of noise stress!

(Before I tell you some of the things I included on my list, you could stop right here and make your own. It might be very enlightening.)

Here's a sample from my list: The alarm clock, baby crying, teakettle whistling. The dishwasher, clotheswasher, or dryer running. Washer and dryer both stopped (another load can go in). The dog whining to get out—or barking to get in. Doors closing, doors opening.

Running water (you've got to investigate this sound when you have small children), the toilet flushing, the toilet running too long after flushing. Boys arguing (when is it serious enough for me to intervene?), boys fighting, one boy crying. Lisette playing with her squeaky crib toy (meaning she is awake).

Television noise, radio noise, stereo music. The electric garage-door opener or car doors slamming. Squealing tires on the street in front of the house always brings an instantaneously stressful stab of anxiety. The vacuum, the blender, the oven timer, the electric can-opener. The car running smoothly, or that odd noise under the hood.

Giggling children in the back of the house. Or absolute silence where children were giggling moments ago. (This last one can prompt reactions varying from an amused "Uh, oh. What are they up to now?" to a sudden panicky "Did they somehow get the medicine cabinet open?") Maternal response to silence varies depending on past experience and the kind of day you've had.

Checking back over my list I realized many sounds in my world carried a double whammy of stress. Almost every appropriate mechanical noise required special attention on my part to make sure that the appliance was indeed operating properly and wasn't making some inappropriate noise. For example, I had to listen for the tell-tale clicking in the dishwasher that told me the sprayer arm was hitting a plastic tumbler which had bounced out of place. And there was the thwump-thwump-thwump of an out-of-balance spin cycle on the washing machine. Or there is the irritating whine and clatter that tells you the vacuum is scarring a rare 1910 dime which dropped out of your husband's coin collection or (more likely) you've risked the health of your Hoover by failing to see a worthless paper clip that's been stuck in the carpet under the dining room table for months.

I could go on with my list. But you get the idea! Everywhere I turned, everywhere I looked, everywhere I listened, I found a noise that added a little (sometimes a lot) to my stress.

Just realizing how much noise stress filled my life was a life-changing revelation for me, I shared my insight and my list with Gregg as soon as he got home that day. Knowing the cause, I no longer worried about my ears bothering me.

Not that they quit bothering me. With five active children in the house, lasting peace and quiet is merely an elusive dream. (Some days I can imagine heaven with optional sound-proof rooms you can stay in for an hour or maybe a century at a time, just for the sheer sensation of peace.)

Recognizing the reality of noise stress has enabled me to control some of it. For example, when my ears bother me, I postpone noisy activities like vacuuming the carpet or blenderizing vegetables for supper's soup. I used to invariably turn on radio music the second I started the car; now I often opt for silence as I drive if my tired ears seem to need a break. Unlike some of my friends for whom television offers a constant friendly voice, our TV is never on unless there's a show we care enough about to sit down and watch. And my children are now programmed to know that when their mother announces, "My ears hurt!" that's their cue to lower the volume and try to find something quiet to do for a while.

There are, of course, some noise stresses that must be endured. The cry of a baby held in your arms is as loud and as piercing a noise as the sound of a pounding jackhammer at twenty feet. Crying is the leverage God gives infants to ensure their needs are noticed and met. Yet while listening to a baby's crying is a natural requirement of motherhood, it's stressful nonetheless. And so are many other sounds that add up to create that sometimes hidden, but always present, stressor: noise.

Hidden Stressor #3: Waiting

Last Wednesday morning my three oldest children were in school. Benjamin, my three-year-old, was at our church for the weekly mothers'-morning-out program. With only five-month-old Jonathan in my charge, I planned to get a dozen errands run all over town in one continuous morning-long rush. And I did it.

By noon I had a head of steam, a morning's worth of momentum. Maybe, just maybe, I could pick up Benjamin, and, if we hurried, manage another couple of errands before we headed home for nap time. I grabbed the baby and we raced up the church steps to Benjamin's second floor classroom. He gave me an open-armed, beaming welcome that would melt any mother's heart. But he wasn't quite ready to go. He had to finish coloring his picture. Then he had to find his morning art project and put on his jacket. We were almost out the door when he decided he had to go back and give his teacher a good-bye hug. Finally we got out the classroom door, down the hall, to the stairs.

In the stairwell I encountered two other mothers who looked like they'd had a morning like mine. They seemed all charged up, eager to go, their body language like that of runners at the starting line—leaning forward, ready to take off. But in front of them on the stairs were their preschool children, descending ever so s-l-o-w-l-y. One step, pause. Another step, pause. One mother, with a look of utter frustration on her face, just shook her head and said, "You just can't hurry three-year-olds can you?"

The second mother and I smiled, each of us shaking her head resignedly. We'd been there before. Every mother has. Because waiting is a big part of every mother's job description—and waiting is stressful.

In chapter 2 we looked at the job stress that results when there's a lack of control. Waiting is time out of your control.

If a mother could save up all the minutes, all the hours she spends waiting for her children and put that time to a single use, who knows what she could accomplish? She might earn a Ph.D., find a cure for cancer, or run for president. Instead, she waits.

I sometimes wonder if all children suffer the same anatomical abnormality mine do. I occasionally declare in exasperation, as my mother used to declare to me, "I don't think you have a hurry bone in your body!"

We wait for children after school. We wait for kids to get ready for school. We wait for them to come when we call them to supper. We wait for them to decide to eat the supper we fixed. We wait for them as they search the closet for their dress shoes five minutes after we should have left for church. We wait for them to finish basketball practice. We wait for them to come home from dates. The occasions seem countless. It's all time out of our control. So it's all stressful.

And if waiting for our children is stressful, waiting *with* our children can be even more stressful.

We found a wonderful pediatrician when our oldest son Andrew was born. The man had a great reputation, a terrific way with kids and parents, plus his office was only two blocks from our apartment. The problem was, I never, ever sat in his waiting room for less than an hour before a nurse finally ushered me into an examining room to wait some more. (Have you ever noticed that the time you spend waiting in a doctor's office is directly proportionate to your child's feelings of discomfort and irritability and inversely proportionate to the amount of sleep you got the night before?) I soon changed pediatricians. Though I drove thirty minutes to the appointment and another thirty minutes to get home, the fifteen minutes I averaged in the new doctor's waiting room made the stress trade-off worth the drive.

And it's not just *my* doctor either. I wasn't surprised to read somewhere recently that pediatricians and obstetricians have the worst record for waiting-room times in the entire medical profession. While I'm not so cynical as to accuse doctors of deliberately deciding a mother's time isn't worth anything, I do suspect this may be an unconscious outgrowth of an irritating societal attitude that says: Mothers can wait.

Think about it. When do grocery stores open the fewest cash registers and allow checkout lines to grow the longest? During the day when the typical customers are retired people and homemaker-mothers—two groups of people who supposedly have time to wait.

It's this sort of cultural failure to recognize the stress of waiting that makes waiting one of the biggest hidden stressors of motherhood—a major stress for most mothers.

We'll look at more hidden stressors in Chapter 10.

10

More Hidden Stressors

There are many other hidden stressors for mothers that don't have direct parallels with other jobs. Not every mother experiences them all, at least not to the same degree. But in talking to women from around the country, it's my guess most readers can relate to most of the following stresses:

Hidden Stressor #4: Relationship Responsibility

As a young woman, Alice had met and married John, very much against John's mother's wishes. John's mother hated the fact that her Protestant son had married a Catholic girl. She constantly criticized Alice for everything from her housekeeping to the large family Alice and John had—doting on her oldest grandchild and pretty much ignoring the rest. As a result, extended family relationships were always strained in spite of Alice's continual attempts to make peace and rebuild bridges.

Eventually, John's mother developed serious health problems—becoming an invalid who needed regular attention and care. John did what he could for his mother, but it was Alice who assumed primary responsibility and made sure her mother-in-law's needs were met.

Why did the responsibility fall to Alice? Why would she work so hard for so many years on a relationship that seemed so hopeless? At the risk of sounding stereotypical here, it's this: Women usually assume more responsibility for relationships than men do. Whether it's in our natures or in the way we are nurtured, women tend to be more relational than men. Because relationships are so important to us, we assume responsibility for making and improving them. And our concern isn't limited to our own relationships; we assume some responsibility for the relationships of everyone around us.

For example: Who's responsible for remembering to send birthday cards to both sides of the family? Who takes the lead in developing neighborhood relationships and friendships? Who becomes most concerned and involved in trying to diffuse sibling rivalry? When marital troubles arise, who raises the issue and/or is the most willing to seek help? The answer is usually—women.

Another case in point—this time from my recent experience. We had lived in our new neighborhood only six months and I still didn't know any of my neighbors very well. But one woman who seemed like a potential friend was the mother of Tony, a boy the age of my Andrew.

One Sunday afternoon Andrew and four neighborhood kids were playing in our yard. Looking out the kitchen window, I saw Tony and a slightly older boy engaged in a tug-of-war over a hula hoop they each wanted. Since they weren't hurting each other, I just watched, waiting for them to work it out. Suddenly Tony gave up the tussle and angrily stomped off—heading for his house. Andrew went running after him to ask him to stay, but Tony just kept going.

I spent the rest of the afternoon thinking about Tony and wondering: *Should I have intervened? Should I call his mother to apologize and express concern that his feelings were hurt?* I did feel Tony had reacted too sensitively to a simple dispute. Yet I wanted Andrew and Tony to be friends. And I'd like to be friends with his mother. *If I call, will I be overreacting to an insignificant childish quarrel? If I don't call, will Tony's mother think I've been insensitive to her son's feelings?*

That one little incident, insignificant in itself, added an unwanted stress to my life that day because it was tied to the bigger issue of relationships. And whenever we assume psychological responsibility for building, maintaining, or repairing any relationship, good or bad, ours or someone else's, it requires effort. That effort adds stress.

Hidden Stressor #5: Financial Responsibility

Whether or not the husband is the primary breadwinner in the family, most mothers serve the role of chief purchasing agent. Even when a husband writes the checks for monthly bills, it's almost always the mother who's in charge of buying food, clothes, and medical service. So even if it's Dad who balances the checkbook, it's Mom who has to make sure it does balance.

All those comedians' jokes about the "keepers of the pursestrings" aside, most mothers take this part of their role very seriously. Just as we mothers assume an emotional responsibility for the state of the family health (chapter 3), we also often assume an emotional responsibility for the state of the family's finances.

A memorable example was shared with me by a mother of two preschoolers whose husband worked for a company known for its below-average pay-scale. Some months the family strained to make it from paycheck to paycheck.

"One day," this mother recalled, "a neighborhood kid came to the door to collect on a Jump-a-thon pledge I'd made for the Heart Association or something. She said I owed her seven dollars. I thought I owed her only half that, but I'd misread the pledge. She was right. And I didn't have seven dollars to give her. I scrounged around the house and finally came up with it, but it took our milk money for the week. I remember giving it to her, closing the door, and just bawling. I'd made a stupid little mistake and it cost us $3.50 we didn't have."

Rich or poor, assuming responsibility for family expenditures places an added, hidden stress on motherhood.

Hidden Stress #6: Entertaining

I recently read a magazine article about First Lady Barbara Bush. She said when they lived in the vice president's residence in Washington, her husband George would regularly call home late in the afternoon to say he was bringing an ambassador, a couple of senators, a Supreme Court justice and a cabinet member (or some variation of that mix) home for dinner and a lively political discussion. Mrs. Bush didn't seem to mind her husband's impromptu dinner parties; it must have helped to have a staff of stewards carry out the last minute preparations. But surely some days the prospect of such surprise supper guests must have caused her at least a little stress.

Even those of us whose idea of a powerful guest is the local school's PTA treasurer find entertaining stressful. Whether we're crowd-loving extroverts or born recluses who invite people over only because we (or our husbands) feel obligated, entertaining creates extra work for mothers. And that means stress.

As one mother said, "I constantly feel swamped by the regular requirements of my teaching job, my kids, my husband, and my home. The preparation needed to entertain company wipes me out for a week."

Preparing to entertain isn't the only source of stress. Many mothers wish they could, or believe they should, do more entertaining. And their dissatisfaction creates a sense of stress.

A constant entertainment-related stress for me is this: My house seldom looks presentable enough for company. One afternoon, just the other week, an old family friend who lives in the town we just moved to stopped by the house to say hello. Fortunately, I was on my way out the door to pick up my children at school and had a legitimate excuse not to invite him in. I apologized for my rush and warmly asked him back another day. Thankfully, I didn't have to invite him in the side door to walk past the crumb-covered table, the breakfast and lunch dishes piled beside the sink, the mound of debris I'd swept to the middle of the kitchen before I'd launched a fruitless search for the dustpan. Nor did he need to walk into the great-room where the toy-strewn floor looked like a Fisher-Price swamp and where a half-dozen loads of clean laundry rested on every available sitting place, just waiting to be folded.

My house seldom looks worse than it did that afternoon when I lucked out. But too many days it doesn't look much better. And rare indeed are the days when a friend, neighbor, or even a vacuum cleaner salesman could show up at my door without causing me to cringe a bit before inviting them in.

Although I've consciously come to terms with the fact that regular clutter is part of the price I pay for mothering five young children, there remains a constant underlying inner tension. Most of the time I wish my house looked more presentable.

Hidden Stressor #7: Little Guilts

We're not talking here about the mother who says, "If only I'd known the Heimlich Maneuver my little boy wouldn't have choked to death" or "If only I'd known more about her friends, maybe my fourteen-year-old daughter wouldn't have gotten involved with drugs." A lot of mothers wrestle with huge, horrible "if onlys." And there's a lot of stress there.

But here we're talking about the little, sometimes almost miniscule guilts. These little oughts and shoulds are so tiny any one of them by itself seems hardly worth mentioning. But the truth is, all those minor guilts added together become a major hidden stressor for many, if not most, of the mothers I've interviewed. Here are a few sample confessions:

"I feel guilty that my family gets fast-food burgers, chicken, or pizza three or four nights a week. But after a tough day at the office, I just don't feel up to cooking."

"I don't need Dear Abby's regular reminders to convince me; I know prompt thank-you notes are important. But I've got a half-dozen notes I still haven't sent for baby gifts. And my little girl is over six months old."

"I should have remembered my brother's anniversary. I feel guilty I didn't even call."

"I have a box in my basement full of my kids' stuffed animals that need tails sewed back on or seams repaired. I know I ought to find an afternoon to fix them; one bear has been in that box for over a year now."

"My oldest son so much enjoyed the baby book we put together when he was little. My second son has a few pictures in his. I keep thinking I ought to get some pictures in my daughter's baby book. But what really makes me feel bad is realizing I didn't even buy a baby book for my fourth child until he was three."

"I ought to get up earlier so we can have a more leisurely breakfast before we all leave home in the morning."

"I should (pick one): be more patient and not be so quick to yell at my kids; put up the wallpaper I bought for my daughter's room last year; read more to my children; get to work on time more often; attend more PTA meetings; talk to my daughter about menstruation; write checks to pay the bills tonight; all of the above."

The list could go on. And it does. And with it comes stress.

Hidden Stressor #8: Phobias

One single mother with two young children had gone through an ugly divorce. She described her first panic attack this way:

"Walking down the aisle in the grocery store one day I suddenly broke into a cold sweat. I couldn't think of anything but getting out of there. My mind raced: *You gotta get out. You gotta get out. You gotta get out.* I couldn't think. Except the same terrible thoughts again and again. *You'll never see your kids again. You'll never see your kids again.* And then: *I can't drive home. I can't drive home. I can't do it. I can't do it.*

"I didn't know what was happening. All I knew were those negative thoughts echoing again and again in my mind. After a few minutes they did finally quit. And of course I did get home; I did see my kids again. But I couldn't go in a grocery store again for months because I was so terrified it would happen again. Even now, years later, there is still a fear in back of my mind that says, 'What if it happens again?'"

Very possibly this women's panic attacks were, at least in part, a result of the combined stress she faced as a single mother raising two children alone, as a professional in a demanding job, and as a vulnerable woman who still had to deal with a disturbed ex-husband who continued to threaten and try to dominate her and her children. But after the first time she suffered an attack of panic, the fear of the next attack, and the recurring panic attacks, themselves, became major stressors.

Any fear creates stress. And phobias (unrealistic fears or unrecognized avoidance patterns) can create a lot of stress made worse by the fact that those who suffer from phobias usually try to hide the problem or don't recognize it at all.

Some phobias have roots going back to childhood: for example, a fear of insects or of thunder and lightning. Some phobias may be symbolic. For example, a fear of crowds may indicate a struggle or concern over lack of identity. A fear of heights might symbolize a fear of failure. A fear of doctors might indicate an unwillingness to face one's own mortality or maybe symbolize one's fear of losing control. Causes and implications vary. Often psychiatrists disagree on the meanings, sources, and strategies of response.

But whatever the case—whether it's a mild claustrophobia which occasionally causes you a little uneasiness when you take your baby and his stroller into an elevator, or a full-blown case of agoraphobia that sends you into a cold sweat every time you even think about walking out the front door of your house—phobias cause stress.

They result in stress whenever and wherever you face them. And trying to restructure your life to avoid these stressors can be just as stressful.

Hidden Stressor #9: Life Events

Most of us have seen those self-rating stress surveys that show up from time to time in newspapers and magazines. Each entry on a long list of life events is given a weighted point value ranging from high stressors—100 points for the death of a spouse, 73 points for a divorce—through moderate stressors—36 points for a change in career, 29 points for a son or daughter leaving home—down to smaller stressors—12 points for the Christmas season and 11 points for a traffic ticket. You add up all the points for events occurring in a certain period of time, say the past year. The higher your total stress score, the greater your chances of serious illness or depression.

I can speak from personal experience on this hidden stressor because I feel as if I've lived much of the past 12 months right in the middle of one of these life-event stress lists. First there was pregnancy (40 points), then an interstate move (20 points but it seemed like more), a new family member (39 points), change in financial state (a move will do that—38 points), new mortgage (31 points), a pinched nerve that put me flat on my back for weeks (53 points), and my five-year-old began school (26 points). A number of life changes resulted from the birth of our fifth child: a change in work responsibilities (29 points); revision of personal habits (24 points); change in work hours or conditions (20 points); change in sleep habits (16 points). Our move from Illinois to Georgia also had a ripple effect on the life-event pond: a change of schools (20 points); change in recreation (19 points); change in church activities (19 points); change in social activities (18 points); and because we're closer to family now, a change in number of family get-togethers (15 points). We squeezed in a short vacation (13 points) and celebrated Christmas (12 points). I found no stress rating for book deadlines, but it seems to me birthing a book is at least as stressful as birthing a baby.

Just thinking about the past year makes me want to take an extra dose of vitamins with iron! But it's also given me a wealth of material for this book. And it's convinced me beyond a shadow of a doubt (if I ever had any doubts) that every changing life event adds to motherhood stress.

Hidden Stressor #10: Spouse Stress

We may not stop to realize it, but any and all stresses on our spouses also add to our own motherhood stress.

One woman told me about her husband's recent battle with insomnia. Doctors had tried unsuccessfully to find a physical cause. There was a lot of pressure at his job; perhaps the insomnia was a result of his own job stress. Whatever the cause, his stress added to hers. She talked about trying to keep their three kids quiet on weekends and evenings when her husband attempted to nap. And she tried to protect him in other ways as well. "I don't know how much to tell him when one of the kids has a problem at school. I don't want to add to his stress!"

Does she protect him from knowing about a problem she'd like to discuss and have him share? That means an added burden for her and less of a shared bond with her husband. Or does she tell him and risk increasing the stress of insomnia on her husband and the family? The dilemma she faces is itself stressful.

I interviewed mothers who talked about the multifaceted stress resulting from an out-of-work husband. There's also a lot of stress on wives and mothers whose husbands are unfulfilled in their work or find themselves stuck in jobs that can't provide for the family's needs.

One woman whose husband was putting in extremely long hours to make the family business succeed, found herself trying to fulfill the role of mother and father to her preadolescent son who desperately needed a male role model. The stress of that challenge and her own feelings of failure and inadequacy as a mother to her trouble-making boy finally prompted her to seek therapy.

Motherhood stress is a big enough topic without trying to cover the often-related subject of marital stress. So I'll only acknowledge that marriage and marriage relationships often add greatly to motherhood stress. There are plenty of good books on the subject and thousands of marriage counselors better qualified than I to give guidance on this subject.

Stresses on our spouses or stresses in our relationships with them can result in added, sometimes hidden, stress on us.

Hidden Stressor #11: Family Variables

Tolstoy's famous opening line in *Anna Karenina*, "Happy families are all alike, every unhappy family is unhappy in its own way," isn't completely true. Every family is different, and those differences often make for different stressors.

Her number of children and their closeness in age can affect how much or what kind of stress a mother feels. Having five babies in nine years has meant my motherhood stress has some different characteristics from that of my mother who spaced seven children out over nineteen years. While I've experienced the stress of being pregnant with and/or nursing a baby for all but a few months of the past decade, my mother had the blessing and challenge of at least one preschool child in her home for twenty-four straight years. I wouldn't argue that one situation is any more stressful than the other, just different.

And then there are differences in the temperament of children themselves. Children with personalities completely the opposite of a mother's can present a stressful parenting challenge. Yet sometimes the bigger problem is knowing how to handle the child who so exasperatingly reminds us of ourselves.

We don't even get to pick the personalities with which our children are born. And that's another area in which we are faced with a lack of control.

Family living conditions and financial status are other variables that can affect stress. Rich and poor families find some stressors in common and others that are very different.

Even the part of the country you live in can be a stressor variable. I find it so much less stressful getting a carload of small children dressed in light jackets and out the door on a Georgia winter day with the temperature in the 40s than I did bundling the entire crew in layers of sweaters and snowsuits, hats and mittens, and driving them to school on a 10°-below-zero day in Chicago. But then I now face a different stress of fighting mildew in the long, hot months of Georgia summers. So there always seems to be a trade-off.

The stressors are as varied as the family's circumstances.

Hidden Stressor #12: Special Stresses

There are, of course, families with a special burden of stress. For example: families with handicapped children; families with a member (any family member) who is chronically or terminally ill, chemically dependent, or emotionally troubled. Physical, sexual or emotional abuse each creates its own stress. And so does marital conflict.

Volumes have been written on each of these special stresses. There's little we can add in this book—except the reminder that any of these special cases automatically multiplies motherhood stress.

Hidden Stressor #13: Wanting It All Now

One day recently I decided to relieve a little motherhood stress by browsing through some of the antique shops in our town. I didn't intend to buy anything; I was just window shopping.

In the back corner of one store I happened upon a gorgeous antique organ. The proprietress immediately noticed my interest and came over to play it for me. The organ's tone was beautifully rich and full. The piece looked in excellent shape. And the price seemed incredibly low for what looked to me to be a valuable antique.

I exclaimed to the owner about how nice I thought it was, and I told her, truthfully, that I might be interested in owning such a piece some day. Right then, however, I didn't have the money to spend on something like this that I didn't really need. A look of friendly concern passed over the woman's face as she hastened to tell me, "You know my daughter sells cosmetics as a way to earn extra money. Maybe you'd be interested in talking to her about it?"

I politely thanked the woman and told her I didn't think I was interested. But I thought to myself, *Just what I need. One more thing to complicate my life.* As I drove away from the store a few minutes later, I thought about that lady's reaction and realized it epitomized a pervasive attitude in our society which says, *If you want something, there's almost certainly a way for you to get it. Why wait?!*

Perhaps it was only because I was in the middle of this book, but I thought there might be a connection between our culturally ingrained disdain for delayed gratification and some of our motherhood stress. How much stress could we avoid in our families, our marriages, and our own lives if we turned down and tuned out of the American Dream? What if we worried less about buying snazzier cars, bigger homes, and the latest in computerized electronic gadgetry?

Perhaps I'm doing what some old ministers do when they say, "Now I've quit preachin' and gone to meddlin'." But if we're honest, I think most of us will have to admit that some of the things we want for our families and for ourselves probably add, directly or indirectly, some hidden emotional and/or financial stress to our lives as mothers.

Hidden Stressors Plus

There are, of course, countless other stressors impacting the lives of mothers. You may be able to name a baker's dozen of your own.

Similar stressors affect different people in very different ways. Where noise stress seems a constant stress in my life, some other stress may be the one that regularly drives you to the very edge of sanity.

But all hidden motherhood stressors, those I've mentioned and others you might list, combined with the more obvious stresses discussed in chapters two through eight, paint a convincingly clear picture. Motherhood is one super-high-stress job.

And if we want to survive it with our sanity and our health, we need to acknowledge the stress, recognize its effects, and develop a strategy for coping with it. That is what we're going to look at in the next part of the book.

Part II

MOTHERHOOD STRESS:
Finding Encouragement and Hope

11

What's It Doing to Me?

The mother of two teenagers told me: "There is a certain security in having your role defined. But my role is less and less defined as my children get older.

"For example, I was to drive my teenage son on his first real high school date the other night. I know I'm the chauffeur. But how much am I supposed to say as Nate's mother? Should I ask him if he found out when the girl's curfew is? If he's got the banquet tickets? Or if he's done this or done that ahead of time? I finally decided that since he was old enough to be dating now, I'd take a low-key approach, sit back, and just do what he asked me to do.

"But it was time to pick his date up and Nate wasn't even dressed. He'd been playing basketball and had forgotten all about the time. I continued to play it low-key as he rushed around getting ready. We got halfway to the girl's house and he discovered he'd forgotten the tickets, so we had to come back home for them.

"This was a double-date, so I had four teenagers in the car. How friendly was I supposed to be? Should I talk to the girl? Should I just keep quiet and drive? No one tells you these things!

"Nate forgot to bring money to pay for photos they had taken at the banquet. He also forgot to ask the girl's curfew. It got to be five minutes before she was supposed to be home and she had to call her mom to come pick her up from the party.

"By the time I got Nate home I was asking myself, 'Did I do my job as a mother tonight?' I didn't feel like I had. But I'd had no idea what the expectations were for me. The entire experience was so stressful that I came home with a terrible headache."

The mother of one infant told me, "I'm a teeth-clencher. When I start getting stressed, I clench my teeth and I can feel the tension go straight up from there. I kept going to a dentist when my little boy was three or four months old. I told him, 'I know there is something wrong.' The dentist, the father of two himself, finally realized what was going on. He suggested I keep a toothpick in my mouth around home. He said when I'd start to clench my teeth, I'd feel the toothpick. Then I should try to relax and decide what had triggered the teeth clenching."

She eventually decided, "The constant responsibility gets to me more than anything else, always feeling as if there's something going on I have to pay attention to. I still clench my teeth but I'm getting better."

The common stresses these two mothers felt, unclear expectations and constant responsibility, resulted in two common effects—headaches and teeth-grinding. But these are by no means the only physiological effects of stress reported by the women I've talked to about the challenges of motherhood. We'll look at other effects of stress here.

Good Stress, Bad Stress

Dr. Hans Selye, often called the "father of stress" because he first established the physical relationship between stress and disease, said, "Complete freedom from stress is death." The point he was making was that stress is by no means always bad; sometimes it's an essential element of human survival.

Selye was the scientist who identified and defined what he called the General Adaptation Syndrome (GAS), the response a body makes to the stressful demands placed upon it. This syndrome, which may be triggered either by something happening around us or within us, is our body's God-given system for the emergency activation of both the nervous system and the endocrine (hormonal) system. It's the process by which we prepare ourselves for "flight or fight." That's good.

And it works like this. Whenever we perceive any "threat" or unusual demand, our nervous system sends out stress messages: 1) from the brain through the motor nerves to the muscles of the body, preparing them for motion; 2) from the brain to the autonomic nervous system which increases blood pressure, heart rate, and blood sugar level, releases extra red blood cells to carry more oxygen to muscles and slows intestinal processes (all for increased energy efficiency); and 3) from the brain to the adrenal gland which sends adrenalin into the blood stream providing a general stimulant for the entire body.

While this is happening, stress messages are also sent by the nervous system to the emotion control center of the brain, the hypothalamus, which is turn triggers an entire second system of responses—the hormonal or endocrine system. This system works more slowly than the nervous system, but its effects last longer in the body. This chemical-control system affects the various glands of the body—pituitary, the adrenal cortex, the thyroid and others—that in turn regulate everything from white cell counts to a woman's reproductive cycle.

The same General Adaptation Syndrome that sends a mother racing into the street to snatch her tiny child to safety also gives an exhausted mother the energy to push her baby into the world at the end of a long, grueling labor and then provides the exhilarating surge of joy and euphoria she feels as she cradles that newborn in her arms. So the GAS is a wonderfully versatile system. And that's good, too.

But it has major drawbacks that are central to understanding the negative effects of stress. Our stress mobilization system is nonspecific—it triggers the same bodily preparation in response to any strong demand—whether the stress is long-term or short-term, requires action or restricts action, whether the source of the stress is positive or negative. And the GAS is primarily a short-term system designed to prepare the body for life-saving action. So when stress doesn't last long, the system works great. It charges the body to maximum power and efficiency and then allows time for the body to rest when the stress recedes. But when the source of stress continues over a period of time, with no time for the system to return to normal for rest, the body begins to show signs of "bad stress." (And because much of our motherhood stress is both long-term and beyond our control, it's "bad stress" on both counts.)

In the short run, the GAS sends energizing signals to the body's skeletal muscles. But over time, constantly energized muscles become fatigued. In the short run, the GAS prepares all the glands and organs for flight or fight. But the same signals, if they remain constant over time, eventually exhaust the body's organs and glands. In the short run, the GAS releases hormones that raise energy production. But the long-term effect may be to create a chemical imbalance that may affect the body in any number of negative ways.

Common stress-related symptoms which can result, include not only headaches and bruxism (tooth grinding), but also:

- heartburn (hyperacidity)
- swallowing difficulties (esophageal spasms)
- insomnia
- hair loss
- diarrhea
- constipation
- memory impairment
- neckache/backaches
- cold sweats
- nausea
- dizziness
- chest pains
- urinary frequency
- muscle spasms
- rheumatoid arthritis
- skin disorders
- hyperventilation

- cardiac arrhythmia
- and much more

According to *Prevention* magazine (September 1987) "stress is being increasingly linked to the development and course of cancer, high blood pressure, heart attacks, diabetes, asthma, allergies, ulcers, colitis, alcoholism, smoking, obesity, headaches, backaches and many other diseases."

If that doesn't sound serious enough, *Prevention* also said, "Recent surveys show that from 75 to 90 percent of all visits to primary-care physicians are for stress-related disorders." Estimates are that American business loses $150 billion a year as a result of stress-related absenteeism, diminished productivity, medical costs, and employee turnover.

Double Trouble for Women

The effects of stress we've talked about thus far in this chapter are equally applicable to men and women. The General Adaptation Syndrome isn't at all sexist. Women can experience all the same physical effects of stress men have. And then some.

But women are blessed with three wonderful and complex physiological processes that have no parallel in men: menstruation, pregnancy, and menopause. All three can affect, and/or be greatly affected by, stress.

The chemically complex reproductive system is principally governed by two master glands—the hypothalamus and the pituitary. And both of these glands are seriously affected by stress. Which means stress can affect women in all the ways mentioned above, plus it can result in any number of symptoms related to the female reproductive system—from PMS to infertility to sexual dysfunctions to post-partum depression to menopausal complications. And many of these symptoms create added stress which creates more symptoms which leads to more stress and more symptoms. (For a more detailed discussion of the various effects of stress on the female reproductive system, see *The Female Stress Syndrome* by Georgia Witkin-Lanoil.)

"Take Two Valium and Call Me in the Morning"

Various studies show that women experience all the negative effects of stress men do—even in terms of health problems such as heart disease, which is more often thought of as a male problem. For example, in a Framingham Heart Study, women in high demand/low-control clerical jobs (a potent recipe for stress) had two times the risk of heart trouble of the average woman.

"And yet," according to Dr. Witkin-Lanoil in *The Female Stress Syndrome*, "when women complain of these symptoms of tension and stress, they tend not to be taken as seriously as men are. Whereas men are given serious tests and treatment for their ailments, many physicians still prescribe tranquilizers for women or tell them, 'Go home and try to relax. Your problem is just stress.'"

Or as Dr. Holly Atkinson wrote in *Women and Fatigue*, "Women's symptoms are more often attributed to psychological inadequacy, while men's symptoms are more often thought to be the result of organic illness."

Why the discrepancy? Part of the answer may be explained by what L. S. Fidell wrote in a 1980 edition of the *Psychology of Women Quarterly*: "Stereotypic notions about women are reinforced in medical school training, textbooks, and medical advertising. Little attention is devoted to female sexuality, and women's psychological illnesses and the need for mood-modifying drugs are emphasized." The unconscious bias of their training may explain why doctors are thirteen times more likely to prescribe tranquilizers for women than they are for men.

And tranquilizers prescribed to relieve stress can create added problems. Tests conducted at Harvard Medical School have shown that commonly prescribed tranquilizers can sometimes lead to an increase in aggression which may appear only when people are involved in frustrating or stressful interpersonal relationships. Doctors refer to this as the "paradoxical" action of tranquilizers. And, according to Donald Norfolk, author of *Executive Stress*, "Many cases of baby battering are now attributed to this phenomenon. Mothers may give vent to their pent-up aggression when tranquilizers loosen their inhibitions."

I'm not saying you shouldn't go to a doctor if you're exhibiting symptoms of stress. There are, of course, other causes for many of these symptoms besides stress, some of which are serious enough that they need to be ruled out. But if another cause can't be found, you need to be prepared for what may be a very unsatisfying, perhaps even condescending diagnosis of: "Just stress!"

As Dr. Reed Moskowitz, the Director of Stress Disorders Medical Services at the New York University Medical Center, warned, "Seventy-five percent of all visits to a physician are for stress-related illnesses, but often, stress isn't something a doctor will even discuss." So you're going to have to find other help.

What Do You Do with Stress?

Before we can control stress, we have to know what's causing it. For only when we see legitimate causes of motherhood stress, can we accept the validity of our feelings of stress.

Even pioneer stress researcher Dr. Hans Selye recognized the therapeutic value of knowledge when he said, "The mere fact of knowing what hurts has a curative value."

Understanding stress is the necessary starting point for successfully coping with it. And it's doubly important when we're talking about motherhood stress—an unrecognized arena. That's why we've spent the first eleven chapters of this book providing this "understanding."

While *stress education* is a first step in coping with stress and can actually reduce stress itself, the next step is *stress management*. And that will be the focus of the remainder of the book.

12

Taking Care of Myself

A friend who leads a large weekly Bible study for women at her church told me this story:

"A young mother of three small children came to me recently saying she needed to talk. So we got together at a nearby restaurant for coffee and a piece of pie. Obviously she felt under great stress. Her exact words were, 'My life is totally out of control.'

"She felt since she was 'just mothering' she at least ought to be able to keep her house in order, which often meant staying up till one or two in the morning to finish doing everything that needed to be done. So, of course, she was almost always exhausted.

"Eating was another problem. She had gained weight, which made her spiral of depression even greater. She didn't like the way she felt or looked.

"When she finished telling about the stress she was feeling my first advice was: 'You need to start by going to bed! You need a regular bedtime. And regular meals. Your body and what you give to your children are much more important than housework. When your children grow up, they won't remember whether or not your house was clean. But they will remember a happy, healthy mother.'"

* * *

We've looked at several motherhood stresses we can't do much about. For example, a new mother has no more control over when her newborn son will overfill his diaper and need a complete change of dry clothes than a mom with a twenty-five-year collection of Mother's Day cards has over who her college-grad daughter will marry (or if she will marry).

And yet we shouldn't feel so paralyzed by all those things in motherhood we can't control that we simply surrender to stress. True, motherhood, by definition, creates stress. And there may be many things about our circumstances, our family, or the demands of motherhood we can never predict or change. But there's much we *can* do to combat and reduce motherhood stress by taking control of our own lives. And we certainly don't want to add to our stress by failing to look after our own basic needs.

Unfortunately, too many mothers I've talked to learned this lesson the hard way. Like the mother my friend told me about, they compounded their stressed-out feelings by taking care of everyone but themselves.

From Yawn to Dawn

Suspended in what often seems like a perpetual state of drowsiness that has lasted for over ten years now, I find myself wondering some days if motherhood is merely a cosmic sleep-deprivation experiment intended for the amusement of the angelic hosts. It all started for me early in my first pregnancy when I had to fight sleep by walking around our apartment as I studied for my graduate school courses. (I still dozed off on my feet from time to time.) And it's continued until this very morning at 6 A.M. when my second-grade son turned on the television so loud he awakened the baby and brought a sudden, unwanted end to what had been a world-record (for the Lewises anyway): a three-wet-beds night.

I've learned from long experience that my feelings of stress are directly related to the amount of sleep I get (or don't get). And unlike some people, my husband included, who seem to function quite well on six to seven hours of sleep a night, I need at least seven and a half (eight is even better) hours or I can feel the stress beginning to build as the day wears on and I wear down.

According to Dr. Merrill M. Mitler of the Association of Sleep Disorders Centers, "Each person has a genetically determined sleep requirement. As far as we know, this need doesn't change during adulthood and can't be reduced by practice."

In other words, the demands of motherhood don't lessen any mother's need for sleep—which means if we hope to maintain our health and sanity while successfully coping with all the stress in our lives, we're going to have to get however much sleep our bodies need.

Sarah told how she did it when her teenagers were younger. "I realize I'm a better mother if I get eight hours of sleep—I just know that about myself. So I refuse to be a martyr. I don't stay up to clean house or do anything else. I go to bed and take care of myself.

"When I'm feeling particularly stressed, it's usually because I'm tired. So I go to bed early."

Another mother seconded this advice: "Once my kids were in bed for the night, I'd get a book to read and go to bed myself. If something wasn't done before bedtime, I told myself it didn't need to be done. I knew I had to get my rest or I wouldn't be able to cope the next day."

A mother with four kids told me, "I just can't function without a full night's sleep. And if I have to wake up enough to get out of bed and take care of a child in the middle of the night, my mind clicks on, the adrenalin starts pumping, and I lie awake for two hours knowing the whole next day is going to be shot." When it got so bad this mother told her husband she didn't think she could handle the stress and the exhaustion any longer, he suggested a solution. "Now we have it worked out so my darling husband gets up with the kids 95 percent of the time. Sometimes he won't hear them and I'll have to wake him. But I can go back to sleep if all I have to do is say, 'Glen! Wake up!" He has no trouble getting up, doing whatever needs to be done, then coming back to bed and dropping off to sleep again as soon as his head hits the pillow. He realizes it's worth it in the long run in his relationship to me, if I get enough sleep."

Whatever changes have to be made, mothers need sleep to cope well with stress. Shakespeare evidently understood the positive effects of sleep when he wrote, "Sleep . . . that knits up the ravell'd sleave of care . . . . sore laborer's bath, balm of hurt minds, great nature's second course, chief nourisher in life's feast." One mother, using very modern words, called it "preventative maintenance. You take care of yourself by seeing that you and your children get enough sleep and are eating properly. That really cuts down on stress."

Beyond Peanut Butter and Jelly

One mother of four kids—ages 4 to 16—admitted: "I used to stand at the kitchen counter after I fed my kids lunch and just nibble at things. So even if I ate something, it always felt rushed. Now after I get the kids situated, what I've started doing is to sit down at the table, eat, and even look through the newspaper after the kids are done. There's a big difference between standing up and eating lunch and sitting down to eat—even if you consume the same food. It's a better, more relaxing break."

At least this mother had been eating something.

When I recently attended a luncheon of mothers who have young children, I overheard a number of comments to this effect:

"It's sure nice to eat lunch for a change."

"I know what you mean. All Billy wants for lunch is peanut butter and it just doesn't seem worth it to fix myself something."

"I never eat lunch either. I just look at it like a special diet."

After research and interviews for this book and years of interacting with mothers of small children—first as an educator and now as a mother myself—my best guess is that the majority of mothers, particularly those at home with small children, get little or no nutrition at lunch time. (And many don't eat nutritiously any time.)

Poor nutrition can actually create stress. And good nutrition can improve a person's resistance to the negative effects of stress—whatever the causes. So eating right, and regularly, can be one of the simplest, most productive ways we have to cope with motherhood stress.

A big part of eating right means getting enough vitamins. And "enough" may mean more than the FDA's Recommended Daily Allowance. A body under stress uses more vitamins; some tests show two or three times as much Vitamin C is needed by people in stressful situations. So maintaining our health under stress may well require vitamin supplements to our diet.

This is something of an aside, but our children's diet can also play an important part in our motherhood stress. I learned this lesson early because, as a preschooler, my oldest son had an intolerance for a commonly used red-food dye—a common childhood allergy. About twenty minutes after he'd ingested anything red—candy, jello, fruit punch, even pink medicine—he'd become physically fidgety and emotionally wired. He'd find it difficult to be obedient and impossible to sit still. In the process of watching his diet, I became very aware of what research has shown for decades—that many of the foods we eat can have a direct effect on moods, energy level, and even behavior.

Despite all that's known and all you can read about nutrition, I'm amazed at how many mothers in already stressful situations—shopping, at church, or other settings requiring added control—will give their kids such sugar-loaded treats as candy, soft drinks, marshmallows, and pre-sweetened cereals—almost guaranteeing added stress when the child's blood-sugar high reduces self-control at the same time it provides a surge of excess nervous energy. Smart nutrition for our families (and for ourselves as mothers) can greatly reduce some unnecessary motherhood stress.

Body Language

Science is proving the effectiveness of a new/old antidote for stress which doesn't come in pill form and can't be injected. Research suggests it can reduce anxiety as effectively as mild tranquilizers. And it doesn't have any bad side effects either. Sound too good to be true? It's exercise.

A lot of mothers think, *Exercise! You've gotta be kidding. I can hardly stay on my feet until I get the kids in bed at night. I certainly don't have the energy for exercise!* I've said the same thing myself. But the truth is, even though you burn energy to exercise, in the long run (and not so long at that) exercise produces more energy than it consumes. It increases physical energy reserves, tones the system to use energy more efficiently—and the invigoration that results often carries over from the physical body to the mental/ emotional, spiritual, and social aspects of life as well.

For a long time we've known and accepted the influence of the mind on the body, but we've been slower to see how the body affects the mind. Researchers still can't say exactly how it works, but they've come up with plenty of evidence that the connection does exist. Some scientists think it's the result of an exercise-induced release of endorphins—a brain chemical that seems to produce a felling of well-being.

Exercise also increases a person's sense of control by providing a means of moderating stress levels. It uses up excess adrenalin produced during stress. And exercise can also act as a healthy distraction from pressures that are building up.

"You have to be willing to take time out for yourself," says one mother of two grade-schoolers. "I didn't do that at first. But right now I'm taking an ice skating class at a nearby rink and I'm loving it."

If you're out of shape, or like me, just not particularly athletic or competitive, exercise can have an ominous sound reminiscent of unpleasant past experiences in junior-high P.E. classes. But it needn't be like that.

For me, the simplest, cheapest, most natural exercise is also a wonderful stress reducer. It can be done anywhere, takes as much or as little time as you have, and requires no special equipment.

It's walking.

When our daughter Lisette was a baby, we spent a week at the beach with my family. My sister Joan had developed an evening walking routine. During that week, I accompanied her on her walks up and down the beach, as a means of spending time with her. It was so easy, so much fun. When I returned home, I began walking after supper each night. Sometimes I would put Lisette in a baby backpack and do my brisk walk with her on my back. Other times I would leave all the children with Gregg.

I could hardly believe how relaxing it was to be out of the house, doing something physically exerting. And it gave me so much energy. I would return with extra enthusiasm and energy to tackle the evening routine.

Another body-over-mind exercise doesn't burn any calories but works well for me when I'm feeling particularly stressed. I draw on all those memories from my natural childbirth classes—breathing and relaxation techniques—to calm my tense muscles and my frazzled nerves. And while this isn't a permanent solution to long-term motherhood stress, it can give me a sense of temporary control which allows me the time to gain perspective and marshal my reserves to cope with stress's immediate demands.

* * *

In earlier chapters we've already discussed the physical demands of motherhood. Trying to tackle them without first taking care of yourself is inviting stress. And in the long run, everyone loses.

It seems so obvious I almost hesitate to say it. But experience and observation tells me many mothers need to hear it: *Taking care of yourself physically needs to be a high priority if you have any hope for surviving motherhood stress.*

13

Taking Care of Mind and Soul

Mothers are more than physical creatures. If we're going to truly take care of ourselves, we need to attend to more than just our physical health.

Mind Matters

Repeatedly mothers told me they had to learn for themselves, often by trial and error, how much less stressed they felt when they took steps to attend to their own mental and emotional health. Again, it seems so obvious. But many mothers still don't do it.

When time always seems like gold and everyone around you has so many needs you want to meet, perhaps it seems a little selfish to think, *I'm going to do something just for me.* But if you listen to the testimony of the mothers I've talked to, a little such "selfishness" may be one of the most generous things you can do for your family.

As one mother of two told me, "I saw a woman's T-shirt recently that said, 'If mom's not happy, no one's happy!' It's so true!" It's certainly not much of an exaggeration. And if we want to be happy, not only do we need to build up our physical reserves with good health habits and exercise, we also need to do whatever we can to replenish our emotional and mental reserves."

One mother, whose college daughter is now studying overseas and whose son has just started high school, said, "When my children were little, I had a grandmotherly lady from down the street who came to take care of them once a week so I could go to the library and read. I looked forward to that time every week because I knew it was mine. It wasn't time to go shopping, because to me that produced stress of its own. It was just my time to relax."

The same mother has revised that practice as her children have grown. She shared the ways she now finds short breaks for herself: "Every morning that I work I drop my son off at school and rather than rush back home to get dinner started or do something else, I stop at a little coffee shop for thirty to forty-five minutes, sit quietly, and spend time by myself. Sometimes I write a letter to my daughter, or read, or do my nails. But it's time just for me before I have to go to work and give myself to other people. I may have to get up a half-hour earlier on those days to do it, but the time for myself is worth it.

"And once a month I go to a flea market. No one else in the family likes to go. So I go by myself. And I have a ball roaming through the barns.

"And sometimes, on Sunday afternoons, I drive out to a lake in the country and watch the ducks. And I'm a much happier person when I come home to join my family. I don't do it all the time, obviously, or it wouldn't set well. Just now and then.

"But I find when I take a little time to do something 'just for me,' I'm much more able and willing to do things for others. It makes me a more willing giver."

Another mom, with a one-year-old baby, said to get any relief from the stress she feels, she too has to find time for herself: "I feel better getting up at 5:45 A.M. and having a shower and a cup of coffee before my little one wakes up. In some ways that adds to the stress, because I'm not getting as much sleep. But I find it's worth it and relieves stress for me if I'm already up when he awakes and needs me. That's my time."

A mother with four kids—a preschooler, a second-grader, a middle schooler, and a high schooler—told how she finds time for herself: "Mini-vacations! I think a lot of mothers have those days when they think, *If only I could get away for a while!* And when you feel that way, you usually can't actually take off for a day or two. You can't just take off for a week at the beach somewhere. But you can take a mini-vacation.

"I'm talking mini-mini here: five or ten minutes. You get these golden moments, and they are almost always unexpected. You may not be able to plan them, so you have to watch for them. Suddenly you realize the baby is asleep, the kids are all playing a game, or there is absolute silence in the house. Take advantage of that. Consciously relax your body and say to yourself, 'Hey, I'm on vacation.' Maybe it will last two minutes and maybe you'll get ten.

"I usually keep some cross-stitch or the latest issue of *Reader's Digest* on the front seat of my car. So when I have to sit in the car and wait, if I'm picking kids up after school or whatever, I take a mini-vacation. Instead of sitting there feeling stressed as I wait and thinking, *Where are those kids? What's taking them so long?* I say to myself, *Hey, I've got five whole minutes to read 'Life in these United States.' This is a mini-vacation.* It changes something stressful to something positive.

"Or say you take your kids to the park and they're climbing on the playground stuff. Sit down on a bench, relax, and let yourself take a mini-vacation. Then after a few minutes you can get up and go chasing after the kids.

"When I take these little breaks it's a way of pacing myself. Instead of pushing all day long until everything is done, everybody is in bed, and then crashing, I find five minutes here, ten minutes there, and do a little crash. It's a great stress reliever!"

A friend of mine, the mother of four daughters under twelve, does the mini-vacation bit on a somewhat grander scale. Every three to six months her husband presents her with a gift certificate for a one-night stay at any of a variety of the nicer hotels in their metropolitan area. (Many hotels have special reduced weekend rates.) He stays home with their kids while she has thirty or so straight hours all to herself (usually from Friday afternoon until Saturday evening) to relax and do what she wants without anyone else's demands interrupting her plans. She spends her freedom reading, setting goals for herself as a mother and wife, sometimes even making a to-do list for her husband, and wandering around local malls without having to look at her watch or having anyone announcing they're tired and want to go home or they need to go to the bathroom "right now."

Both she and her husband feel the investment in time and money pays multiple dividends for their family and their marriage.

But even if you don't have the time, money or a husband willing to brave thirty hours of solo parenting, you could try from time to time to get away from home and the burden of responsibility for a day—or even a few hours. You'd be much better equipped to deal with the stress when you got back.

There's a lot to be said for the benefits of exercising your creativity, too. Gardening and handicrafts may be solitary pursuits, but they are emotionally/mentally relaxing. They can actually increase a person's self-esteem by providing success experiences. And mothers certainly need those.

I don't find as much time to do it as I used to, but I enjoy cross-stitch. And in trying to analyze why, I've come to the conclusion that it appeals to me (as it evidently appeals to many mothers) because it's one of the few things in my life that can be done perfectly and stays done. I get a sense of completion and control that is always missing from my stressful life as a mother. Gardening, too, provides some of those missing elements that result in motherhood stress; for example, proof of success comes much quicker and is a lot more measurable when you're growing roses or tomatoes than when you're raising kids.

While rest, relaxation, and recreation were cited by many mothers as recommended, stress-reducing roads to better emotional and mental health, some mothers also said they found working outside the home helped reduce some of their motherhood stress.

Of course, as any mother who's ever worked a paid job can tell you, doing so adds to stress in other ways. But there are trade-offs which many women pointed out.

A mother with an eighteen-month-old son said, "I don't

have the stress of isolation because I work two days a week [as a pharmacist]. It gives me a chance to get out and it keeps me from forgetting what I went to school for so long to get. I enjoy my work, so that relieves some of the monotony I feel at home sometimes.

"And I actually rest more at work than I can at home. At home I'm constantly moving, but at work I occasionally get all caught up. Then I can sit down and drink a cup of coffee and not have someone asking me a dozen questions or pulling on my pant leg or something."

A mother of nine- and six-year-old-boys said her sometimes stressful part-time job as a public health nurse helped her cope with her motherhood stress. "It gives me a chance to talk with adults. I get the satisfaction of doing something for others. And unlike my job as a mother, it's something I get regular positive feedback on," she said.

I too found numerous stress-relieving benefits when I taught one or two college classes a week. (Though one was much better than two, and I always felt extra stressed on the days my classes were scheduled.) My outside work provided a type of mental stimulation I didn't get from listening to my children read from their easy readers. I got to talk to real live adults face to face. Positive student feedback provided a boost to my ego. And teaching college gave me a sense of status I didn't always feel when I was scraping petrified baby cereal off the underside of a high-chair tray.

I have to admit that of the women I talked to, those most likely to cite a beneficial stress/relief-of-stress result from their outside work were mothers employed in part-time jobs. Those with full-time outside jobs more often felt their dual mother/employee roles added more stress than they relieved.

While my interviews were by no means a scientific sampling, my findings dovetail pretty well with a recent Gallup Poll commissioned by *Newsweek* to determine women's views on work, motherhood, and feminism. While a majority of all mothers, employed and nonemployed, said that given a choice they would prefer to be employed (82 percent of those already employed and

71 percent not employed) only 13 percent of the employed mothers and 9 percent of the nonemployed mothers said they would prefer working a full-time job with regular hours. The vast majority in each group expressed a preference for flexible hours, part-time employment, or work they could do at home. And the biggest percentage in both groups (employed and nonemployed) said they'd prefer part-time work.

While I realize a majority of mothers today work outside the home and the biggest percentage of them say they do so because of financial pressures, the option of choice (for those who had a choice) would seem to be part-time employment. And that's because it's the one option that may offer more mental/emotional relief for motherhood stress than it creates.

One more strategy for maintaining our emotional/mental health needs to be mentioned: laughter. Georgia Wiltkin-Lanoil, a mother herself, writes in *The Female Stress Syndrome* that laughter is the signal "to turn off the emergency adaptation system. As Norman Cousins suggests in his book *Anatomy of an Illness*, 'Laughter may even promote healing. What a delightful tool for stress management! . . . It lights up our faces, relaxes our muscles, lowers our sense of vigilance, restores our objectivity, and enhances hope.'"

One hectic afternoon recently, I left Gregg at a baseball practice (he was the coach), and dashed headlong to the local mall to pick up Andrew and Matthew from a birthday party, with the three younger children in tow. Unfamiliar with the mall, I parked in the wrong lot and ended up walking the length of the mall twice, carrying Jonathan and keeping pace with Benjamin and Lisette, before finding my older children. We stopped at a restroom on the way out of the mall. As I waited for the children to finish, I looked at my watch and realized that by now practice was over and Gregg was waiting for me, on a cold spring afternoon. And it would still take me ten minutes to get the children into the car and another good ten minutes drive to pick him up. I couldn't decide whether I felt like crying or screaming.

Until Matthew began telling me knock-knock jokes he had heard at the party. We all laughed as we made our way back to the car. The laughter helped me put it all in perspective: Gregg does not like to wait, but he probably would rather do that than take my place, dragging five children through the mall. And I felt much more like hugging my children than hitting them.

In *Executive Stress,* Donald Norfolk quotes a psychiatrist who observed, "I've seldom been called upon to help a person who had a sense of the ridiculous, and I've *never* had to treat anyone who could really laugh at himself."

If you can't laugh, at least try to smile. Dr. Charles F. Stroebel, medical director of the Stress Medical Clinic of Hartford and author of *QR: The Quieting Reflex,* recommends you "Smile inwardly and outwardly with your eyes and mouth" as part of a regular relaxed response in stressful situations. He says, "This is faster than popping a pill, and you can do it anyplace, anywhere, anytime."

Soul Food

One mother laughed as she talked about her stress in raising two young boys. "My husband says the reason God gives people children is to continuously drive us to our knees. A lot of days I think he's right."

This mother meant to be serious as well as funny. A number of mothers echoed the words of a mother of three young girls who told me, "One of my chief means of coping with stress is prayer."

She went on to give an example, "Whenever I feel ready to blow my stack I try to catch myself, take a deep breath, step into another room where there aren't any kids, lean against the door, and pray for patience. It helps."

A number of women we talked to recommended finding a regular time for prayer, Bible reading, and meditation. And while I know from my own experience this is hard to do, one mother gave good advice when she said, "You can't wait till everything is quiet and all your work is done, or you'll never find the time. You just have to make it a priority."

After living for the first fifteen years of our marriage in

Illinois, we moved last summer to our present home in Georgia. So it's been a year of great and varied stresses. When Gregg and I have felt the most stressed we've often commented that we don't know how other people make such momentous decisions and go through so much turmoil without the peace and strength that comes from a belief in a personal God who cares about the details of our lives.

How do mothers cope with so many things that are out of their control without trusting in a God who is in ultimate control? How do they cope with all the change without believing in something and Someone who is unchanging? How can they live with such a terrible sense of inadequacy without faith in Someone who is all-sufficient?

I couldn't. And I don't. I couldn't hope to cope with my motherhood stress without caring for myself spiritually, as well as emotionally and physically.

Another stress point is connected with spiritual health. Many mothers admit they struggle with stressful feelings of guilt and failure. But we can find encouragement in the Bible's message that we've all failed; we're all imperfect.

"When I know I've blown it," one mother of nine said, "I try to admit my mistake and ask forgiveness if it's needed. Even from my husband and children.

"Then I also pray to God about it. Because I've found forgiveness to be a real stress reliever."

We'll say more about finding support in the next chapter. But I will say here that I don't know how I would cope with my stress as a mother without the fellowship I find through my church—with women who share my faith, know what I'm going through, care about me as a person, and support me with their prayers, their concern, and their thoughtful actions.

It would come as no surprise to many of the women I talked to who cite their personal faith as an important factor in their coping with stress. But no less an authority than Robert Rodale, editor-in-chief of *Prevention* magazine, said, "Many social scientists agree that membership in a religious group has a beneficial effect on the nerves. In fact, researchers are finding out that there's something about a religious lifestyle that contributes directly to well-being."

That's because we humans are tri-dimensional beings with body, mind, and soul. If we want to live a truly balanced life we must nourish all three. In fact, trying to take care of yourself or to deal with stress without including a spiritual strategy is about as futile as sitting on a three-legged stool with one leg missing. Even if you're taking care of your mind and body, I don't think you can find the balance you need to successfully cope with stress without seeking spiritual strength and support.

Taking Control

In addition to being creatures of body, mind, and soul, God created us as social beings. Human beings, mothers included, need the support of other people. And in the next chapter we're going to look at ways mothers can and should be able to find a sense of support and the benefits that result when we find it.

Seeking support is yet another way any mother has for taking care of herself.

14

Hey, I'm Not Alone!

One beautiful early spring Thursday, I loaded my two-year-old and four-year-old into their wagon and toured the neighborhood delivering flyers supporting a local school referendum. We'd been out nearly an hour when we knocked on the door of a friend's house—a couple of streets over from ours.

When my friend Rachel (the mother of two grade-schoolers and a toddler) opened her door, she greeted us warmly and invited me in for a cup of tea. Immediately, I noticed that one side of her face looked red and swollen. But I'd no sooner begun to usher my children inside and ask Rachel how her week was going than she apologetically referred to "this thing on my face. I've had it all week and I finally went to the doctor yesterday. He said it was hives."

"Some kind of allergy?" I asked.

"No," Rachel replied. "He went through a list of questions with me and finally said it was 'just stress.' He told me I needed to go home and take it easy for a while. But it's not getting any better."

As the conversation moved on from Rachel's hives, I thought about some of the stresses I knew she had in her life as a mother. And she began to talk about some of them.

First she told me that her out-of-state in-laws were coming for a weekend visit. Rachel said she dreaded their visit because they were always openly critical of the way she raised their grandchildren. And she gave some examples of the kinds of hurtful, insensitive things they'd said in the past.

In between her telling me a little about her son's recent problems at school and her husband's new work situation that was demanding long hours at his office and overnight trips almost every week, we laughed and exchanged funny stories about our two-year-old's entertaining, but exasperating, behavior. Rachel also proudly showed me around the house to see the new carpeting that had just been installed the day before, as she recounted the disruption of their family life over the preceding seven months since a freak flood had forced them to completely gut and remodel the bottom two floors of their split-level home.

I didn't have to say much that morning. I knew the stress she'd been under, so I just let her talk and merely listened. That was evidently just what she needed, because when I finally got ready to leave two hours later, I was amazed to notice her hives had almost cleared up.

Honest Lives + Honest Words = Real Friends

That experience with my friend Rachel served as an unforgettable reminder to me of the stress-relieving power there is in the most simple acts of sharing, caring, and listening. But that kind of support only happens in an atmosphere open enough to encourage honesty—not just honest talk, but honest actions as well.

I remember either hearing or reading Dr. James Dobson's comment that he thought one of the most unkind things young mothers did to each other was always hurrying around picking up, straightening, and cleaning their houses before another mother came over. And I think Dobson's right. We're not presenting an honest picture of ourselves or our lives to each other. And the result is the kind of comparative performance stress one mother of two described this way:

"I see mothers with more children than I have. And their kids are all taking piano lessons by the age of four or playing the violin and doing a thousand other things. These mothers are involved in leadership roles in church programs and are active in community programs. And they keep their houses clean. And that I *really* can't figure out at all. I don't understand why I can't do all they do. I have fewer kids and fewer responsibilities.

"I feel like a terribly inadequate mother. I compare myself to them and I come up very, very short."

I find the intensity of this mother's feelings both disturbing and comforting. Disturbing because she's a dear friend who's as terrific a mother as any woman I know; and if such a professional, mature, sensitive, and self-assured person as my friend could feel so much acute performance stress, most mothers have to feel it even more intensely. But I also find her words comforting because I know our relationship fostered no false pretenses to add unnecessarily to each other's motherhood stress. Neither of us ever felt the need to shovel up the clutter before the other one dropped by. And the openness and honesty which illustrated and symbolized our relationship were primary factors in making it a supportive and stress-reducing friendship.

One mother, whose two children are almost grown, summarized what mother after mother told me when she said, "The most helpful thing I ever found for dealing with my stress as a mother was my friendships with other mothers. I wish as a young mother I had taken more time to develop friendships. I don't know why I didn't. Maybe I was just too wrapped up in the newness and the stress of young children. But I didn't learn until later how important such friendships are."

A mother of two small boys said, "When it's nice weather I often go outside in the afternoon. And my backyard neighbor will see me and come out to talk at the fence. That's our 'wailing wall.' She talks about her seventh grader and the latest thing he is doing to drive her nuts. And I talk about what kind of a day it's been for me. Sometimes we talk about what we plan to have for supper. But we always seem to talk about what we didn't get done.

"My neighbor is the one person I can cry with in the afternoon. I don't feel I have to put up my guard with her. I don't know what I'd do without her."

Such backyard friendships are becoming an endangered species in our modern American lifestyle. Many families move so often and live such hectic lives they don't have time to meet their neighbors. And with the majority of mothers working outside the home, even many young-family neighborhoods look like ghost-towns during the day when over-the-fence friendships might develop.

Yet I've found good alternatives to face-to-face friendship. Before I moved from Illinois last year, my best friend Judy and I went out to lunch together. As we ordered our food, we laughed at the realization that in ten years of intimate, supportive friendship, our good-bye lunch was the first time the two of us had ever gone out alone—without kids or spouses—to do something together. We lived only blocks apart, babysat regularly for each other's kids, and dropped by frequently at one another's houses. But our primary interaction came by telephone. For years we talked an average of two or three times a week on the phone, sometimes an hour or more at a time, about the stress we faced in our lives as women, wives, and mothers. And we both found such great support through our mutual friendship—knowing when we felt stressed out we could always reach out and touch someone we knew would understand our feelings.

"Understanding" is one of the chief stress-relieving benefits of friendship cited by mothers I talked to. Another benefit was expressed this way by a mother of two teenagers:

"I also draw tremendous affirmation from friendship. It's so easy as a mother to feel you're valued because of what you do for the people you serve. Friends love me for who I am more than for what I do. They help give me a real sense of value as a person. And that is a stress-reducer."

Another big plus mothers said they got from friendship was the sense that they weren't alone in their experience or feelings. A mother whose oldest daughter had recently left home for college talked about the stress she felt about giving her daughter up to adulthood:

"I wasn't prepared for the pain of that separation. I guess a lot of mothers don't talk about it and I haven't seen much written

about how that causes stress. But I'd walk by her empty room and
just sob and sob. I drove somewhere in her car, opened the glove
compartment, and saw her sunglasses. I had to pull off the side of
the road until I stopped crying. Or I'd pull into the driveway at
night and see the windows to her room dark and it would hit me:
She's not here anymore.

"When you carry a child and even all those years after
they're born, they are a part of you, part of your life. Then
suddenly they're gone. The severance seems so traumatic. I think
it may have been the worst experience of my motherhood because
I wasn't prepared for it. And that caused stress. I wondered, *Am I
normal?*, and that caused more stress.

"It wasn't until I started talking to other mothers with
grown or almost-grown children that I realized many mothers
evidently go through similar feelings. But we don't talk about it
very much. Maybe we're afraid of seeming too sentimental or too
possessive toward our kids. But if we'd talk and understand the
feelings are normal, we'd relieve a lot of stress."

A number of mothers told me they find a reassuring sense of
normalcy through participation in some sort of support group.

A mother with two of her own biological children and two
adopted kids recalled: "A few years ago in a Bible study I attended,
another mother brought up a problem her child was having. And
one of my children was having exactly the same problem at the
same time. I can't describe the sense of relief I felt. I was normal! I
wasn't alone!"

A mother of five- and three-year-old boys said, "I can be
having a really stressful time and I can go to a meeting with other
mothers, say at church or at my oldest son's school, and just talk
about mother things. And I realize everyone else is just like me;
I'm not the only one having trouble coping with this or that. And
it puts my stress back in perspective.

"For a while I went to a local support group called Mother
Center which was part of a national group headquartered in
New York. There was even a syllabus we'd use to get together
and talk about various child-rearing issues—toilet-training, or
night-walking or some other problems many mothers have.

"I always felt so good after going to those meetings. It was always the same group of mothers, which was great. After talking to those moms about their experiences, I'd come home from each meeting thinking, *Now I can make it through another week.*

"If it wasn't for the chances I have to get out and be with other people, especially with other mothers, I'd definitely be stressed out."

Mothers who don't have a support group like this can usually find one. Most local churches have either mothers' groups or other meetings of women—Bible studies, women's clubs, etc.—where a number of mothers regularly get together and often talk, at least informally, about motherhood issues. A lot of towns have LaLeche League meetings as support groups for nursing mothers. There are numerous local organizations for Mothers of Twins or mothers of children with many other kinds of special needs. Churches are a good place to call and ask about local resources and support groups. You can probably get information on LaLeche League contacts through local hospitals, public health agencies, or any group providing natural childbirth classes. And a call to a local LaLeche League official or a visit to a meeting could give you other leads on the kind of support groups available near where you live.

If you feel the need for help in coping with your motherhood stress, and you don't have a regular support group, try to find one. Based on personal experience, I'd suggest visiting more than one group until you find the one that fits your individual needs for help in coping with motherhood stress.

Ask for Help!

Just having supportive friends or finding a good support group will help relieve some of the general motherhood stress you experience. But they may not always be enough to help you cope with specific stress.

The good advice given by one mother of four I talked to was, "Don't be afraid to ask for help when you need it!"

She suggested a number of elaborations on that advice, including this testimony to her own experience:

"Find another mother and set up a trade-off system. When my oldest daughter was little, I had a friend with a child her age and we each took each other's daughter once a week. That way, when one of us was sick or needed some extra time, the other one would take her child. My daughter was familiar with and comfortable in her home, so it wasn't hard to ask for help. The arrangement evened itself out over time and we both had a regular period we could count on for a break from kids."

But don't just ask friends for help. Don't be afraid to let anyone who has reason to care about you and your family know when you need their support. Starting with your husband.

Husbands Can Be Helpmates, Too

Remember Marlene and Tim, the parents of triplets? Marlene became so stressed and depressed by the lack of feedback she was getting about her mothering that she began to wonder whether or not Tim even loved her. She said, "I became so discouraged that one night when Tim was gone I wrote him a letter telling him exactly how I felt. Then I went to bed, leaving the letter on the table where I knew he'd see it when he got home.

"I never expected the letter to hit him so hard," Marlene said. "He cried and apologized, saying he hadn't realized how I was feeling. He assured me he loved me and appreciated all the things I did. We stayed awake crying, praying, and talking about a lot of things that night."

Both Tim and Marlene admitted that was a turning point in their lives, in their marriage, and in Tim's response to Marlene's motherhood stress. And it happened because Marlene took the risk and asked for help.

Some women I talked to were reluctant to ask for stress-relief from their husbands. They thought their husbands wouldn't understand or had enough stress of their own to carry.

An interesting recent survey of female readers conducted jointly by *Woman's Day* magazine in the United States and a monthly Soviet magazine called *Krestyanka* found that a consensus in both countries believed women have too much work and too little help from their husbands. Other studies have shown that even as more women have begun working outside the house, men are doing little to provide additional help around the house.

Yet despite all this bad news suggesting a shortage of support from husbands, I heard many encouraging stories about sensitive, supportive men who responded wonderfully when they understood their wives' stress and were asked for help.

There was a California mother with four small children who told her husband, "If I could just have some time to myself every Saturday morning, it would make my week." He was more than willing to supervise the kids, so they don't have to pay for a babysitter. And the kids watched cartoons then anyway. The mother takes her Bible and a journal and goes to Denny's to eat breakfast and have a couple hours all to herself. Her husband has gotten into the routine and enjoys the time she's gone. And she looks forward to that time all week and knows she can count on it.

And remember the two examples in chapter 12? The husband who volunteered to take over night duties when his wife told him she couldn't get back to sleep when she got up with the kids? And the husband who gives his wife coupons for a one-night's stay in a local hotel and takes care of the kids so she can get away by herself for up to thirty-six hours?

Sometimes a husband's support can be seen and felt in smaller things. As in the case of a first-time mother (with a fifteen-month old) who said, "My baby's getting older now and things are starting to fall more into place. There are fewer days like there were in the beginning when I couldn't say I'd accomplished a single thing besides caring for the baby. So my husband Rolf learned pretty quickly not to ask, 'What did you do today?' In fact, he sometimes comes home now and notices something I have done to comment on. That's a whole lot more supportive."

But getting stress support from husbands, just like getting it from friends, requires a mother to admit her feelings of stress openly and honestly, and ask for help. For those men who need a little extra persuasion, there's a special chapter for husbands/fathers at the very end of this book. Written to men, by a man, it succinctly covers much of the ground this book covers. It's included so women can ask their husbands to take just a few minutes and read it—sort of a crash course in the causes, effects, and implications of motherhood stress aimed at raising sensitivities and encouraging yet a higher level of support.

Holy Help

It bothers me that some of my feminist friends—and too many professionals involved in daycare and early childhood issues in this country—haven't given churches their due. You can build a pretty strong case for saying the Christian community, and local churches in particular, have done more in the way of support for women and mothers than any other single institution in America. A majority of this country's day-care programs and/or facilities are provided by churches. More mothers'-day-out programs are sponsored by churches than by any other institution.

And nearly every local church has a variety of programs in which wives and mothers find fellowship, strength, and practical assistance in meeting the specific needs and stresses in their lives. Right now I find a lot of enjoyment and sense of support that comes from shared experience at a women's circle meeting at my church which meets monthly for a short Bible study over a bring-something-to-share salad lunch. And at the church we attended in Illinois, our couples' Sunday school class routinely provided a stress-relieving week's worth of meals every time a family had a new baby.

Admittedly, there are no more perfect churches than there are perfect people. And the Christian community in America certainly has its flaws. But if you're looking for meaningful help in coping with motherhood stress, there's no better place to begin than in a local church.

That isn't to say the church couldn't do more. The church, and often the evangelical community more than others, is quick to proclaim a commitment to family values and cite the glories of motherhood (at least every second Sunday of May and in any discussion of the Equal Rights Amendment or women's lib), but often there is more rhetoric than recognition of the realities of motherhood and motherhood stress.

For example, if a minister served a church where 50 percent (or even 25 percent) of his congregation was made up of people from one profession—say medical doctors, teachers, or auto assembly-line workers—he'd almost certainly take some specific steps to inform himself about the demands on, and the work of, that group. You'd expect him to regularly make some related reference in his sermons, and to consistently recognize and respond to the common needs of that group in all aspects of his ministry.

Yet how often does your minister affirm mothers by including realistic illustrations from motherhood in his sermons? How often does he try to make an application of his teaching to the everyday life and problems of a mother?

The church could do more to put its money where its mouth is when it comes to de-stressing motherhood. But still, other institutions haven't done as much.

Societal Support

How much do we value and support the importance of motherhood in this country? You have to wonder when Congress debated and watered-down legislation for so long that the United States became the last of the major Western nations without a nationally mandated maternity-leave policy affirming the especially crucial roles mothers play in the lives of newborn infants.

Despite numerous studies showing the long-term benefits (in cost, loyalty, training, etc.), business and industry have dragged their feet in providing on-site day care, allowing flex-time or shared-job options and making other simple adaptations which could ease motherhood stress among working women.

The fact is, most businesses and government policies are still geared toward the husband-bread-winner, homemaker-wife family—which (according to *Newsweek*) by 1986 represented only 10 percent of all American households. "It's just incredible that we have seen the feminization of the work force with no more adaptation than we have had," said former Labor Secretary William Brock. "It is a problem of sufficient magnitude that everybody is going to have to play a role: families, individuals, businesses, local government and state government."

But mothers are not going to get the stress-relieving support they need from any source—whether government, industry, the church, or even husbands, support groups, or friends—until women themselves accept the validity of motherhood stress, honestly admit their needs, educate others as to their stress, and ask for support. When and if we do that, my experience, and that of women I've interviewed, tell me we will find hope and help.

15

Motherhood Stress Relievers

A mother with one baby said, "I read a lot. I didn't know much about babies because I'd never been around any. So I felt like I needed to read just to learn the basics. But there's so much conflicting advice out there you can't possibly follow it all. Trying to only adds to your stress. So I've learned if you think the advice seems reasonable you should try it. If it doesn't sound right, you should just disregard it.

"A friend who has four kids helped me learn this lesson. She listened to me. She never told me to do this or that, but she'd give me lots of suggestions. One time was pretty funny. It was back when my little baby was waking up six times a night. He wasn't hungry; if I tried to feed him he wouldn't eat. Sometimes he wasn't even wet. He just seemed to want someone to come into his room and pick him up for a while.

"My friend had several suggestions, 'You could try this or this or this. And if all else fails, if you know all his needs are met, you could just let him cry.' And that's what we did. First, we went into his room and made sure he was okay. And then we just let him cry until he cried himself back to sleep. After only two nights, he was sleeping through.

"I called my friend to thank her for her wonderful advice. 'It worked great,' I told her.

"*'Really?'* she responded. 'I never had the nerve to try that myself.' We both laughed. I was so glad she hadn't told me that before.

"She also gave me the most wonderful stress-relieving advice on advice when she said, 'Ask all the advice you want, but always remember you don't have to take it.'"

* * *

So that's how I recommend you read this chapter—a sampling of stress-relieving suggestions from me and from women I've known, met, or interviewed in the course of writing this book.

The preceding two chapters focused on what I feel is some of the best overall advice I've found for reducing motherhood stress—the importance of taking care of ourselves and the necessity of finding support. And a prerequisite to those steps is an understanding of the reality of motherhood stress—its causes, its validity, and its effects—which is what the first part of this book is intended to provide.

What's here are some more specific strategies—strategies learned in response to understanding particular stressors. So you might just consider this chapter a mini-support-group meeting where a number of mothers share a hodgepodge of wisdom on coping with motherhood stress.

I suspect some of their strategies might help relieve your motherhood stress, but all I know for sure is they worked for the women who shared them with me. So try what sounds good; what doesn't sound right or doesn't fit your situation you can simply disregard.

Stamping Out Noise Stress

A mother of one high schooler and one college student reported: "When my kids were small I made them have quiet times—partly for their sakes, but also because I needed a time of peace and quiet. Even after they gave up naps, I would just say, 'Read a book now. This is a quiet time.'

"As they've grown up, our quiet time has been seven to nine

in the evening. We don't have the TV on then or allow radios playing. It's their study time. If they choose not to study they can read or do something else quiet. We don't actually ignore each other, but it's not a time for conversation either. The kids go to their own rooms. I need that time. And I think kids need to learn the value of quiet—especially in our noisy world."

Changing Perspectives on Clutter

A mother of four said, "One of my expectations for a long time—since I don't have a 'real' job—was that everything should be perfect. My entire house should be immaculate. My meals should be delicious. And my children should always be well-dressed. There was always that tension.

"But this didn't take into account that we're dealing with real people here—my family and me. For one thing, I don't have the energy level to give my children all the attention they need *and* maintain that kind of standard. And the other thing I've learned is that when you have young children you cannot keep a house immaculate.

"With Lindsey [her adopted four-year-old who's lived with her for eighteen months] it's incredible. I thought my other children were messy! Lindsey absolutely can't stand neatness.

"Friday is my big cleanup day. I have a woman who comes to help me for four hours. We push and do the whole house from top to bottom. And when she leaves I look around and think, *Ahhh! This is how my house is supposed to look.* Then Lindsey comes in and goes, 'AAAch!' It's almost a physical reaction. She'll go over, take a basket of doll clothes and dump it. Then she'll take a basket of stuffed animals and spread them around. And then she'll go 'Aaah' as if, now for her, it looks the way it should.

"I've had to decide that if I don't want to live in a state of constant tension with her, I have to lower my standards even farther than I had before. I have to say, 'Okay, with Lindsey home, this is the way it's going to be.' Fortunately I have a husband who understands that.

"As adults we think, *Who messed this up?* And kids think, *Who picked this up?* We have to realize theirs is a different perspective. And we have to adjust."

Living with Lower Standards

A mother of teenagers said, "I didn't even make my bed yesterday. I had piles of clothes all over our bedroom and my husband thought it was great. So I'm learning I don't have to always have everything in place. There are times when you have to realize other things are more important than housework. You just have to be content with what you can do and with what you can't. For instance, I came home last night, crawled into bed, and thought, *This makes a lot of sense; I don't even have to turn the covers back.*

"Everybody wants some sense of order in their house. But forcing that at the expense of yourself is not worth it. If you haven't taken care of yourself, your physical needs will soon become greater than your need for order. So taking care of yourself needs to be a much higher priority."

A mother with a kindergartener and a preschooler talked about similar adjustments in her attitude toward keeping house. "I used to feel a lot of pressure to have a perfectly clean house. Now I have cobwebs everywhere. Last night in the bathroom I noticed this beautiful spider web up in the corner. As I called my oldest son in to look at it, I thought, *I've come a long way.* I consider it a positive development for me not to freak out over a cobweb."

Know Yourself and Accept Your Limitations

You can create a lot of stress for yourself if you're using someone else's standards to judge yourself. I was reminded of this a few years ago when I had a college student babysit and do light housework for me one afternoon a week.

Since I hate folding clothes and find that to be my biggest

laundry-related stress, I'd do ten loads of laundry the twenty-four hours before my babysitter came and let her do all the folding. One day I was still home when she started and I stood and watched her fold. She was a whiz. Her hands were almost a blur. She finished that mountain of clothes in half the time I could have done it. So the next time I had clothes to fold, I tried to make myself work faster. I ended up a nervous wreck—with poorly folded clothes. I realized I just can't work that fast with my hands. Acknowledging that helped me understand why my clean clothesbaskets sometimes stack up around my family room like jets around O'Hare. Now I don't feel so much stress about the problem and am more willing to ask for help from my children and my husband.

Heading Off Stress at the Pass

A mother of four said, "My basic philosophy for coping is something I picked up from my husband when we were first married and he was trying to teach me about football. 'The best defense is a good offense.' Sometimes you can plan ahead.

"For example, when my oldest daughter [who is now sixteen] was eight or nine, I put a lot of pressure on myself thinking it was my job to keep her entertained. Finally I made up a poster of 'Things to Do when There's Nothing to Do.' We hung it up and kept adding to it, even writing up and down the margins until at last count we had 104 ideas on it.

"Now when someone comes complaining to me 'There's nothing to do around here' or, heaven forbid, 'I'm bored!' (We call that the 'B' word and it's not allowed in our house), I don't have to do anything but point them to the poster. There are all kinds of ideas: Put on a wedding for stuffed animals; write a thank-you note to someone; sharpen all the pencils in the house; clean out a closet; paint your toenails; play a board game; give someone a back rub; make a list of all the things in the house smaller than your hand, etc. Having it all written down ahead of time takes the pressure off me once and for all."

Little by Little

One mother who's had two children of her own, adopted two, and cared for foster children as well, said, "A social worker once counseled us that the foster children we'd be having in our home would have many problems. And they would not be able to work on them all at once. So if I wanted to teach them table manners, I should work on that and just let it go if they forgot to put the top on the toothpaste or flush the toilet. Once their table manners were acceptable, then we could work on toothpaste.

"I've found that advice works for my own children as well. You don't have as much stress if you don't try to teach everything at once."

Focus on Your Personal Stress Times

Identify the situations that create the most motherhood stress for you personally. Ask yourself what stressors are the main problem—noise, lack of control, constant demands, whatever. Then brainstorm possible solutions.

For example, a stressor for me is grocery shopping with a passel of children traipsing along. I've tried to counter that by going when the oldest kids are in school; but there's still the stress of taking a three-year-old and a baby. I can never predict with certainty when a three-year-old will need to go to the bathroom or when a baby will fuss for no apparent reason, so the stress remains. I don't want to shop in the evening or have my husband shop because it takes away from family time together. So I've decided to cut the frequency of my grocery shopping by going once every three weeks and stocking up. I was accustomed to going every week, so it took more careful planning at first. I had to stretch it to every two weeks, then to every three. And I still make quick stops for milk at a convenience store and at a little produce market for fresh fruits and vegetables. But I've cut my number of stressful grocery shopping trips by two-thirds.

You can apply this same kind of problem-solving approach to any of the most common specific stress times and situations mothers shared with me—bedtime, getting kids off to school, etc. Regular stress times often can be improved by following the next bit of advice.

The Routine Routine

Those major stressors—unpredictability and lack of control—sometimes make it impossible to develop and stick to established routines. But when you can establish a routine—according to several mothers—you help eliminate some of that unpredictability and gain a little extra control.

For example, Marge, a mother of four, said, "A few years ago I decided I hated putting kids to bed; it was just such a stressful time. So my husband said, 'Let's take turns.' But things only got worse.

"I watched. Sam's style of putting the kids to bed is as different from mine as could be. He's throwing children up in the air and racing them to the bathroom where they had toothpaste fights. And if they felt like reading fourteen books, he'd read fourteen books!

"The the next night it'd be my turn and I expected them to go quietly upstairs, put on pajamas, and brush their teeth. Then I'd read one book, we'd have one Bible story, say prayers and that was it.

"Trying to alternate and do it both ways just didn't work. We decided there needed to be continuity every night, and since Sam is often gone at bedtime, it had to be me. So I've learned that my kids operate better and with less confrontation and stress when the regular things are done the same way all the time.

"Getting ready for school is the same as bedtime. When you have the routine and kids know what to expect, you eliminate a lot of unnecessary stress."

Reduce Your Stress by Doing More?

We all have a tendency when we're overwhelmed with motherhood stress to withdraw into a survival mode. We think,

I'll do what I can for myself and my family and that's it. But don't ask me to do anything for anyone else. Yet when we adopt that attitude we may be losing out on a surprising source of stress relief.

A recent *Psychology Today* report on more than 1700 women who regularly volunteered to help others, found more than 85 percent of these women reported feeling an "identifiable physical sensation—best described as stimulation—during the actual helping." And in many cases, "This *helper's calm* was linked to relief from stress-related disorders such as headaches, voice-loss and even pain accompanying lupus and multiple sclerosis."

Psychology Today speculated (and cited a scientist who claims he's about to prove it with his research) that this helper's high resulted from the body's release of endorphins, the same pain-reducing chemicals released by exercise. "Although the feel-good sensation is most intense when actually touching or listening to someone," reported *Psychology Today,* "it can apparently be recalled." Over 80 percent of the respondents in this research reported that their *helper's high* would reoccur, though not as intensely, when they remembered helping.

That report seems to have interesting implications for anyone feeling stressed. And it confirms my own recent experience when I've gotten a warm sense of satisfaction and an encouraging boost of energy on days when I've done volunteer story-reading to my children's classes in the public school, or the day I stopped by a local church-supported women's shelter to donate some of my used maternity clothes for a pregnant homeless woman.

I find it encouraging to realize the biblical principle of service for others has immediate as well as eternal rewards. While I can't do everything, I can reach out to others and actually reduce my stress in the process.

You Can't Make Everyone Happy All the Time

One mother said, "My preschool daughter hates to go with me when we drive car-pool for the older kids. Every single day that I drive, I get her in the car and she cries. It used to drive me crazy. But I finally realized while it was my responsibility to be her mother, it wasn't my responsibility to make her happy all the time. I *had* to drive car-pool. If she didn't like it, I was sorry. But she would have to live with it. Once I decided that, I didn't have the stress of guilt I had before."

Find an Organizational System That Works for You

One mother with four kids told me how she'd found a new stress-relieving system of managing her housework. She writes down every household task on a separate three-by-five card and files them by the week, the month, or however often she routinely does that task. It's a sort of adapted "tickler file" system many secretaries use to keep track of routinely repeated tasks.

"When I was sick last winter and couldn't keep up with what needed to be done, I just took the cards out and refiled them—knowing they'd come up again. So the undone things didn't hang over me. For example, when I'd see that the chandelier in the dining room needed dusting, I didn't feel any pressure to stop and do it. I just thought, *I'll get to it when it comes up in my file.*"

When this mother finished telling me about her strategy, I thought, *That sounds so simple. Maybe I should try it.* But then I realized how long it would take me to catalog all the household duties that need to be done. I also realized how much stress that kind of a black-and-white-on-paper system would cause me; it's just not my style. And I quickly decided this mother's system wouldn't work for me.

The experience reminded me that there are many good organizational ideas for household management out there. And they often show a lot of potential for reducing motherhood stress. But I have to pick and choose which elements of what system work for me and my family.

The system that does work for me is a weekly to-do list. I keep it in a spiral bound notebook with a page for each week. On that page, I write the date at the top and then have three columns of things to do: at home, away from home, and phone calls to make. On the bottom seven lines of each page, I have a line for each day on which I write specific appointments or scheduled events. Sometimes a day or two passes when I'm not able to check anything off my to-do list. But usually by the end of the week, I have checked off enough items to feel a sense of accomplishment. And keeping a to-do list helps me keep track of the important things that tend to get lost in the mountains of urgent things I have to do.

But every system has its flaws—as evidenced by a funny story shared with me by a mother of two adult children. She recounted how both of her kids were in diapers at the time she and her husband were doing graduate work at a big midwestern university. Some semesters their daily schedules and academic demands forced them to adopt creative measures for dealing with housework: "The only way we could keep our heads above water was to let the dishes pile up all week and wash everything on the weekend.

"Then one day in the middle of the week some out-of-town friends called to say they were passing through town and asked if they could drop by in a few minutes. Suddenly it was panic time. There was no way to do a week's worth of dirty dishes before the company arrived so we quickly piled the dishes in the bathtub in the bathroom closest to the kitchen in our rented mobile home. And then I closed that bathroom door.

"Everything looked great a few minutes later when the company drove up. Until they came in and asked if they could use the bathroom, and I remembered the tub in the second bathroom was full of dirty diapers. Now I was faced with a dilemma, *Which bathroom do I show them, the one with the dirty dishes or the one with the dirty diapers?* Talk about stress!"

At that point of this mother's story we were both laughing so hard I forgot to ask which choice she made. But I remembered her story as fair warning that not all creative coping strategies always work to reduce motherhood stress.

At Home Escape

"Sometimes I've gotten a babysitter when I didn't have anything planned," said the mother of an infant. "I'd leave him with the babysitter and I'd go upstairs and lock myself away to read a book, cross-stitch, take a long hot bath or do something else I wanted to do."

Focus on the Positive

Another mother said, "If I can just find the little things that are rewarding. If I walk into a room and my little boy wants to show me something he's proud of. If he's snuggling up next to me, I can stop and appreciate the feeling. Focusing on the little positive moments of motherhood reduces the stress."

Asked what advice she wished someone had given her before she became a mother, one woman surveyed for *The Motherhood Report* by Louis Genevie and Eva Margolies wrote: "I wish someone would have told me, 'Motherhood can be very difficult, and there will be times when you wish you never had children. But there are also times when your children will give you such joy and pleasure that all the bad things and feelings disappear as if they never existed. Focus on those times, and they will get you through anything.'"

Words of Wisdom

A number of tid-bits of strategy and insight on stress were shared, noted, or came to mind in the course of writing this book. Here are a few of those:

Wise Word #1 —Don't waste your big guns on little crises. Don't use the same tone of voice to say, 'Comb your hair,' as you would to say, 'Don't lie.'"

Wise Word #2 —Remember how quickly the seasons pass. Many of the stresses you feel today will be gone tomorrow. There will certainly be new stresses, but at least today's will be gone.

Wise Word #3—Sometimes the problem with kids is that they are just so . . . well, childish. We need to have realistic expectations for each of our children for their particular ages.

Wise Word #4—Find a system of discipline that works for you. And then be consistent. "If you don't, you're setting yourself up for stress," said one mother of four.

Wise Word #5—Pray for your children regularly. It's easier to be patient with people and problems when you've been praying. "I like to go in to my children's rooms when they've dropped off to sleep," reported one mother of five. "I'll put my hand on each child's shoulder and pray—sometimes thanking God for something positive I saw that day, other times praying about a need or concern I saw. The night I can do that, I go to bed with a better perspective on my motherhood stress."

Wise Word #6—Don't put off hard decisions; indecision creates stress. Often, making no decision is more stressful than making a wrong one.

Wise Word #7—When stress piles up and the future looks overwhelming, ask yourself, "What's the worst thing that could happen?" Sometimes consciously facing the worst case scenario makes reality seem more manageable.

Wise Word #8—One of the techniques for reducing interpersonal stress recommended by the United States Association for Mental Health is: "Give in occasionally." Sometimes surrender is a very effective stress reliever. Even the bravest generals know you sometimes must retreat if you hope to live to fight another day.

Six-Step Stress Control

In a study reported on in a variety of popular and professional publications, two psychologists formerly at the University of Chicago studied hundreds of business executives to determine what traits best enabled them to maintain their health in the face of severe daily stress. They isolated three important factors. Those best able to cope with stress 1) felt in control of their lives, 2) saw unexpected events as challenges, and 3) were committed to their work.

We'll be considering the implications points 2 and 3 have for motherhood stress in the next chapter. But the issue of control ties in here with a discussion of strategies. Because the researchers who did this study developed a six-step strategy they taught business executives to cope better with stress. Here's an adaptation of those steps for coping with motherhood stress:

1. Try keeping a daily journal or log of when you feel stressed. What stressors can you identify? What patterns do you see?

2. Listen to yourself. Instead of saying, "I can't cope with this today!" encourage yourself: "I know this is stressful, but I'm gonna make it!" Turn your self-talk from negative to positive.

3. Do what you can to relieve the stress now. Any stress that can be relieved immediately needs to be dealt with.

4. Accept those stresses you can't control. A lot of motherhood stress falls into this category. That classic prayer by Saint Francis of Assisi ought to be engraved on every mother's heart: "Grant me the serenity to accept the things I cannot change, the courage to change the things I can, and the wisdom to know the difference."

5. Be consistent when possible. We're talking about routine again here. One study done at the University of Arizona showed that families with regular bedtime and mealtime routines not only had fewer hassles, but the children experienced fewer cases of bronchitis and pneumonia.

6. Keep it in perspective. For mothers, a lot of stress just comes with the territory. You have to weigh the good against the bad.

We'll look at ways to focus on the good in the next chapter.

16

Recapturing the Joy

I enjoy cooking. But sometimes, by the time I get supper on the table, I feel too tired to eat. I'm often exhausted in general and especially tired of whatever it is we are having for supper. My family comes to the table hungry and exclaiming, "This looks good!" And I think, *I've been looking at this, smelling it, and tasting it to see if I have it seasoned right, for the last hour. Now, the last thing I want to do is eat it.*

So each week I always anticipate Wednesday evening—the night the entire family goes to our church to eat supper. I look forward to sitting down to a meal I didn't have to prepare, eating it hot, and conversing with other adults while I eat it.

One recent Wednesday night we went through the line, and my husband got the children seated while I went for water. No glasses were left. So I trudged into the church kitchen in search of plastic tumblers, ice, and water. I'd just finished distributing the drinks when Benjamin spilled his and I had to go get a pile of napkins to mop up the puddle.

After throwing the napkins away, I returned to the table thinking, *I've been pushing so hard all day. At last I can sit down, and my food is still warm.* I took the first bite of my piece of spicy-baked chicken.

"Mama, I need to go to the bathroom," five-year-old Lisette said. "Will you please go with me?"

150

I let out a long sigh, but when I turned toward my daughter her big beautiful lavender-blue eyes looked adoringly into mine. And my heart just melted. *Eating can wait,* I told myself. Then, as we walked from the dining hall to the restroom, Lisette wrapped her arms around my arm as we walked. When she leaned her cheek so sweetly and affectionately against my bare arm, it warmed my soul. My cold chicken dwindled in significance as I thought, *There are no happier moments in life than moments like this.*

Not long after that experience I was talking about motherhood with the mother of three children who told about going with her husband (then her fiancé) for premarital counseling to the minister who was going to marry them. "He asked us if we were in agreement about children," she said. "And I told him yes, we both wanted to have children when we could afford them.

"The minister started to laugh. 'No,' he told us, 'you don't understand. No one can ever *afford* to have children.'

"And you know," this mother said. "That minister was right. There never is a time when you can 'afford' children financially or emotionally. Becoming a mother can never be a totally rational decision because it's never convenient or easy. But it is such a joyful experience!"

And motherhood has other paybacks as well.

As a mother of two boys said, "I think my experience of motherhood has made me a better person and a better nurse. It's made me a more sensitive, understanding professional."

Another benefit I've felt in being a mother is the new understanding it's given me of God. As a mother I can better understand the unfathomable depths of a Heavenly Father's love. When I realize how easy it is for me to forgive my child's wrongdoing, I find it easier to accept God's forgiveness for me.

Certainly the motherhood experience enriches every mother's life. As one woman who didn't have her first child (she now has two) until her mid-thirties said, "We had fertility problems. And I decided—if we had children, fine, but if we didn't, it would be okay. I never felt a burning desire or drive for motherhood. However, it's turned out to be so wonderful I think everyone should experience it. It's just impossible to describe how sweet a little baby can be. I've experienced a whole range of emotions as a mother I'd never known before and would now hate to have missed. It really is a joy."

It's an undeniably stressful job God has given us mothers. But in his infinite wisdom he's also created us in such a way that it's in the very doing of our demanding job where we find both the rewards and the strength to do it. In the last chapter we looked at the scientific search for the explanation behind "helper's high"—the calm feeling of well-being that results from service to others. There's more evidence, according to *Prevention* Magazine (June 1988)—based on studies at Harvard, the Menninger Clinic, and elsewhere—that altruistic acts and feelings of love and caring actually reduce the effects of stress on a human body.

So it disturbs me when I talk to a stressed-out mother who seems to be responding to her overload of stress by pulling back from her children, spending less time with them, and emotionally withdrawing from a level of interaction she's had in the past. While there's much to be said (as has already been noted in chapter 12) about the need for stressed mothers to take care of themselves, caution is needed. Time and again I've seen women whose stress triggers a destructive spiral of mounting stress; she feels stressed out so she pulls back from her involvement with her children. In doing so she reduces the opportunity for those positive stress-reducing interactions, those warm, joyous moments that are perhaps her best source of the strength and encouragement she needs to cope.

So how do we avoid that?

First, we have to recognize the validity and sources of motherhood stress. Then we must find positive ways of taking care of ourselves. If we can also find avenues of support, they may lead to some practical strategies for controlling some of the specific stressors we face as mothers.

But even if we do all that, much of the stress will remain. It's a fact of life for mothers. And much of motherhood stress is forever and hopelessly beyond our control.

So if we're going to survive the stress with our sanity and health intact, we're going to have to consider the second and third factors so helpful to the executives in the corporate research cited at the end of chapter 14. In addition to taking steps to control what they could, those executives who coped best with stress did two other things. They viewed unexpected events as challenges. And they felt commitment to their work. Both these factors boil down to a matter of perspective.

Where do we get that perspective as mothers?

There's an old, old story about three stonecutters at work in a large city square, each with a hammer and chisel, cutting away at his own large stone. A stranger passing through the city stopped in the square and watched the men for a while before wandering over to the first man and asking, "What are you doing?"

"Can't you see?" the stonecutter responded gruffly. "I'm cutting stone."

The stranger quickly retreated and then meandered over to the second stonecutter to ask the same question. "What are you doing?" The second man looked up and smiled, saying, "I'm earning a living so I can feed and raise my family."

Finally the traveler approached the third stonecutter. When he asked his question this time, the worker set down his hammer and chisel, motioned toward the stone he was working on, and proudly told the stranger: "I'm building a great cathedral. This stone I'm cutting is going to be part of a magnificent building, a tribute to God that will last for ages after I'm gone from this world."

Each of these men had a different perspective on the same work. The first stonecutter felt tired, discouraged, and bored by his labor because he focused on the work itself. The second man seemed more content in his work because he realized how his work would benefit him. But the third stonecutter saw his work as part of a bigger picture, full of spiritual significance and lasting importance. His perspective gave him a true commitment to his task.

As mothers, we may be faced with many things we can't control, but we can choose our perspective. Rose Kennedy was one mother who understood the importance of seeing her role in perspective. In reflecting on her life she wrote, "I look on child rearing not only as a work of love and duty but as a profession that was fully as interesting and challenging as any honorable profession in the world and one that demanded the best that I could bring to it."

Whether or not your children or mine ever become president, they deserve just as high a perspective from us as mothers.

This chosen perspective is also part of what I see reflected in an old poem written by Ruth Hulburt Hamilton which was copyrighted and first published in the October 1958 issue of *Ladies' Home Journal*. The last stanza has become a popular verse to use on wall plaques and in cross-stitch patterns. But the rest of the poem isn't as familiar. Yet it holds special meaning for me because I was my mother's fifth child, and because my youngest son Jonathan is my fifth baby. And the poem is titled:

Song for a Fifth Child

Mother, oh mother, come shake out your cloth!
Empty the dustpan, poison the moth,
Hang out the washing and butter the bread,
Sew on a button and make up a bed.
Where is the mother whose house is so shocking?
She's up in the nursery, blissfully rocking!

Oh, I've grown as shiftless as Little Boy Blue
    (Lullaby, rockaby, lullaby loo).
Dishes are waiting and bills are past due
    (Pat-a-cake, darling, and peek, peekaboo).
The shopping's not done and there's nothing for stew.
And out in the yard is a hullabaloo
But I'm playing Kanga and this is my Roo.
Look! Aren't her eyes the most wonderful hue?
    (Lullaby, rockaby, lullaby loo).

Oh, cleaning and scrubbing will wait till tomorrow,
But children grow up, as I've learned to my sorrow.
So quiet down cobwebs. Dust go to sleep.
I'm rocking my baby. Babies don't keep.

No, babies don't keep. I've learned that. I've also learned that caring for babies and watching them grow entails much more than warm images of rocking and sweet cuddles.

I can relate to the story one mother told me about going to church feeling (and evidently looking) terribly stressed. She recalled having three children in tow when, "An older woman stopped me in the church hallway and admonished me to 'Cherish these days, dear. The years will go by so fast!'

"Well," this mother told me, "I wasn't exactly having a day I wanted to cherish. So when I got home from church I called my mother. 'Mom,' I said, 'You had six children. Tell me. Do the years really fly by?' My mother was silent for a long time. And then she said, 'Well, the years do go by fast, but some days last forever.'"

Every mother knows what it's like to have one of those forever days. Or even longer nights.

Motherhood is a tough job. A demanding job. And it's certainly a stressful one.

Discussing their landmark survey of a thousand mothers about their attitudes toward mothering, authors and therapists Genevie and Margolies wrote in *The Motherhood Report*: "Time and again, we were struck by how often mothers wrote poignantly and at great length about the less-than-gratifying aspects of motherhood. Indeed, if one were to measure motherhood moment by moment, the less-than-pleasurable aspects would outweigh the enjoyable ones. Yet this is not how most women experienced the role. Even mothers who found a lot of drawbacks to motherhood, who experienced many disappointments, often reported that they felt motherhood was rewarding. At first, this appeared to be contradictory, a defensive attempt on the part of mothers to hide their true feelings. Upon closer scrutiny, however, it became clear that, although most mothers did not experience the joys of motherhood with the same frequency as the negative aspects, the joys they did experience had tremendous psychic weight, often compensating for the more frequent difficult times."

As an example, these researchers quote one mother who wrote, "For every time you feel frustrated and helpless, they have a hug. For every time they make a mess, there is a smile. For every time they break your heart, there is a kiss and an 'I love you, Mom.'" And after what appears to be a fairly equal balance of pros and cons, this mother concluded, "But in all, the good outweighs the bad a thousand times over."

Motherhood is undeniably stressful. But it's also an almost unimaginable honor and privilege. And I often remind myself of that with a regular ritual I began with my oldest son Andrew and have continued with all five of my children. From time to time I'll pull him aside, look deep into his blue eyes and tell him, "I've got to be the luckiest mama in all the world. Because of all the mamas in all the world and all the little boys in all the world, God let me be Andrew's mama."

Every time I repeat that little litany, I marvel at the wonder of it. It keeps life in perspective as it reminds me that along with all the stress, motherhood also brings unspeakable joy.

But it's only when we begin to acknowledge, understand, and respond to the reality of motherhood stress that the joy can work its magic. It's then we can see that the rewards of motherhood can outweigh the stresses of motherhood "a thousand times over."

Maybe even more.

Afterword: Just for Fathers from a Father

By Gregg Lewis

Burnout. Job stress.

Newspapers, popular magazines, and professional journals have said a lot on these subjects in recent years. Psychologists have conducted studies. Medical researchers have run tests. Sociologists have collected survey data.

The overwhelming conclusion? There is a serious problem with stress.

Concern first focused on high-powered executives. Follow-up research found it among assembly-line and clerical workers. Eventually concern spread to those burning out in the so-called "helping professions"—teachers, counselors, ministers, and social workers.

Over time, students of stress and burnout isolated a number of factors that contributed to the problem of job stress. As you read the following quotes highlighting major sources of job stress, think about those factors that make your job stressful.

"It's just understood that I'm on call twenty-four hours a day. I can't count the number of times I've been needed in the middle of the night. And when I do get a chance to get away on vacation with my family, much of my work has to go with me." *Constant responsibility* is a major factor in job stress.

"Maybe I expect perfection from myself because all the other people watching me expect it. I know I feel incredible pressure to perform." *High expectations and demands* are major job stressors.

"It's not like I can call in sick. No matter how awful I feel, I'm expected to keep functioning at some level." The *physical demands* of a job add to stress.

"My job description changes every week—sometimes almost daily. Every time I turn around someone adds something to it." *An unclear or changing job description* can create serious job stress.

"There's always more to do than there is time to do it. I'm constantly battling against the clock." *Time pressure* is yet another job stress.

"Despite all the pressures and all the skills I'm supposed to exhibit, despite the fact I'm the first one those around me come to when there's a crisis, it's not like I'm getting paid what a lot of my friends are." *Low pay* can often be a job stress.

"Most people are quick to say my job is important. But when I'm at a party or in any kind of public setting and the question of my profession comes up, the questioner invariably turns immediately to whoever's standing next to me to inquire, 'And what do you do?' Few people even know how to talk to me about my job." *Low status* is another job stress.

So too is a sense of futility or a *shortage of options*. "It's not like there is any real opportunity for advancement at this point. I don't feel I can quit. I'm afraid to start over. I just don't know if I could hack it out there in a new career at my age."

One of the most common stress factors in any job has been illustrated by research done on what we might naturally assume to be one of the most stressful jobs around—professional race-car driving. According to Rick Gilkey, a professor at Emory University's School of Business Administration in Atlanta, studies show the greatest stress on race car drivers occurs not while roaring around the track at more than 200 mph, but during pit stops when the pit crew controls things. *Lack of control* then is more stressful than speed or danger for professional racers. According to Gilkey, the same holds true of corporate managers whose firms are being taken over by other companies. When a takeover robs them of assurances and a sense of control, it's like sending them to the pits.

Yet another job stress factor, as important as *lack of control*, was illustrated in the job experience of a good friend of mine. Harold served a few years ago as campaign manager for a candidate running for a seat in the U.S. House of Representatives. He dragged home late one evening from campaign headquarters, feeling exhausted.

"What a stressful job!" he exclaimed to his wife. "And the worst part isn't the long hours or the emotional drain. It's the unpredictability of politics. I started today with a to-do list as long as my arm. Then we got a mid-morning phone call cancelling one of our scheduled events and the rest of the day was up for grabs as I faced a whole new set of priorities. I never know at the beginning of the day how much I'll be able to get done or what crisis is going to disrupt my plans. It's just so unpredictable!"

Unpredictability is a major job stress in any job. But then Harold's wife, the mother of two preschoolers, knew that. She smiled sympathetically at him and said, "I know. Every day is like that for me."

Harold had to admit he hadn't thought about motherhood in those terms before. Most men haven't. But we should.

For not only is unpredictability common to motherhood, so are all the other job stress factors we've listed. In fact, all the above quotes pertain specifically to the job of motherhood.

If we carefully consider all the factors research says make for high job stress, we have to acknowledge the undeniable truth. Motherhood is hard, stressful work.

Most of us would be quick to say we believed motherhood to be important work. But too often we've short-changed our mothers and the mothers of our children by failing to recognize how stressful their job is. We don't very often think of it as work, let alone as a profession subject to the same stresses other jobs present.

Not that men ought to shoulder all the blame for underrating the demands of motherhood. It's often a reflection of a broad societal value which some women, themselves, adopt; you can hear it in the words of many stay-at-home mothers who say, "I'm *just* a mother. It's not as if I work." The clear implication then is that being a mother isn't important work.

The same implication is seen among those mothers who do other work outside the home (over 50 percent of mothers today). They expect, and are expected, to simply fit their mothering tasks in around everything else. As if it can be done any time, with no real effort.

Why do we say motherhood is so important and then not even think of it as a real profession with real job stress? When a mother stays home with her children, why do we so often think of that as "taking time off" to raise children? When a mother also pursues work outside the home, why do we so seldom think of her as a two-career person?

Part of the problem is that we, society in general and men in particular, take motherhood for granted. We have a limited reference point; we observed our own mothers and now we observe the mothers of our children. Growing up we probably didn't think that much about our mothers' mothering; we just accepted it as what mothers do. And most of us know better than to try to compare our wives to our mothers, so we take a similar attitude toward our spouses' mothering. It's what mothers do.

We look at a woman colleague in our workplace and we know how to measure her work in terms of proficiency and productivity. We can't measure a mother's job in the same way—which adds to the underlying attitude that motherhood is different and not a "real" job.

Another reason we underestimate the job stress of mothers is the belief we have that being a mother is easier today than it was in grandma's day. Not true!

In an award-winning study of the practice of housework from the seventeenth to the twentieth centuries, historian Ruth Schwartz Cowan concluded that every major "improvement" in household technology had one (or both) of two main effects: 1) It raised expectations and standards to previously unimagined levels. (For example, doing a load of laundry is easier today. But where our grandmothers brushed dried mud off overalls so they could be worn another few days, if we dribble milk on our shirt in the morning we toss it in the dirty clothes and put on a "clean" one before we leave for work.) Or 2) it shifted more of the responsibility to women. (For example, running water revolutionized household cooking and sanitary practices. But where men and children usually hauled water from a well or spring, carried out slop jars, even dug and treated outhouses, it's almost always a woman's job to scrub sinks, tubs, and toilets.)

The main thrust of all household improvements, according to historian Cowan, has been to free men from their age-old household routines so they can go off to work in cities and factories. The end result is more work for mothers, not less. Especially now when most women have joined men in working outside the home, this "household progress" is taking a big toll. It is, according to Cowan, "a toll measured in the hours that employed housewives have to work in order to perform adequately first as employees and then as housewives. A 35-hour week (housework) added to a 40-hour week (paid employment) adds up to a working week that even sweatshops cannot match."

A couple of recent surveys indicate that men are taking a slightly more active role in helping around the house. But the overall statistics still don't look good. Those men whose wives work outside the home only average an hour or two more per week in "helping out" than those husbands whose wives are home full-time. So it's pretty obvious women are pulling more than their share of the weight when it comes to housework— which is one more reason that motherhood is a tough, stressful profession.

Women's frustration with the workload distribution adds to their stress. In a nationwide survey of mothers documented in *The Motherhood Report* only 25 percent of American mothers were "very satisfied with the support they received from their husbands." The remainder (more than seven out of ten mothers) had two primary complaints. The first, "He doesn't do his share," was predictable. But according to the survey, what bothered many women even more was "that their husbands failed to take any initiative. Couldn't he see there was work to be done? Why did she always have to ask, or nag, or, worse yet, feel as if she was imposing?"

So what can we as fathers do to help our wives cope with motherhood stress?

Obviously, we could try to take initiative and shoulder a bigger share of the load. But that's not enough of an answer. No matter how much we do to help out around home, we can't keep motherhood from being stressful. The issue goes deeper than initiative and workload.

According to *The Motherhood Report* on the feelings of more than a thousand women, "Mothers seem to be saying 'Respect me, praise me, value me, help me.' But many husbands fell short in giving their wives the support they needed. What made the lack of support even worse was the implicit message husbands sent when they failed to wholeheartedly support their wives: 'I do not respect the enormous amount of giving, caring, and loving that you routinely give every day.' In the eyes of these men, motherhood is not only 'The Second Oldest Profession,' as Erma Bombeck called it, but also a second rate one at that.

"The consequences of not receiving adequate support went even deeper, far beyond the resentment an unsupported mother felt. We found that when a man fell short of giving his wife the emotional and practical support she needed and felt she deserved, it negatively affected the whole emotional tenor of family life" in a broad variety of negative ways.

But the same report offered this encouraging conclusion: "With a father's encouragement and support, a woman is more likely to have a closer family, a better marriage, more patience and love for her children and better feelings about motherhood and about herself."

So what can we do to provide this kind of effective support?

Based on what I've learned about the issue of motherhood stress as I've helped my own wife research and write this book, based on my own understanding of job stress and the experience of mothers we've talked to from around the country, I've got several suggestions for us as men that could not only help relieve our wives' feelings of stress as mothers, but could enrich our marriages and improve our family lives as well.

We Can Recognize the Problem

To begin with, we have to recognize the validity of motherhood stress. That's easier to do if we think of motherhood as a profession and consider all the job stress factors that apply. I've mentioned a few of the implications here. But you'd get a much clearer picture if you'd read or scan through the first ten chapters of this book. And then we ought to talk to our wives about the job stresses that bother them most as mothers. Recognizing and understanding stress is the first, perhaps most important step in dealing with it.

We Can Give Feedback

The next thing we can do to ease motherhood stress is something I was reminded of just last night. We had a birthday party at our house yesterday—for four-year-old Benjamin. I helped organize some of the games and even dipped a little ice cream when it was time for refreshments.

When it was all over, Debi and I talked about how much we enjoy kids' birthday parties. And she told me she appreciated my help and complimented me on being "such a good daddy." When I replied that she was "a good mother, too" Debi responded, "Thanks, I need to hear that more often."

And I realized again what I've realized before: I don't compliment Debi on her mothering nearly as often as she comments on what I do as a father. I'm going to try to be better. And most men need to be.

Lack of feedback is a stress in any job. So when we give our wives positive feedback on their mothering, we relieve one stress and at the same time provide encouragement that helps them better cope with other stresses. It's a small, easy thing to do. But giving positive feedback could be one of the most important things we do for the mothers of our children. I guarantee you it will be noticed and appreciated.

We Can Lend an Ear

Understanding the reality of their stress and giving our wives positive feedback on their mothering are certainly two ways we can give support. But another important element of support was illustrated for me recently by a couple of friends. Lynn, a mother of three small children, had spent five straight years either pregnant or nursing babies. She was constantly worn out, and a lot of days she felt tied down.

Her husband Bill remembers the day recently when their youngest was only a couple months old and Lynn told him how tired she felt. How she could never get away. How she never felt as if she had any time to herself, and on and on.

Bill's immediate reaction was, "Then why not quit breast feeding? You'd be able to get away and I could take care of the baby. I could get up with her in the middle of the night and you could get more rest."

At that Lynn exploded, "You don't understand! I don't really want to stop nursing. I know I'm tired and this isn't going to last forever. I realize this is just the stage of life we're in right now, and I know it will get better. So I don't want your advice! I just want to tell you what I'm feeling right now. I just want you to listen!"

Bill says, "I don't know why I'm so quick to give advice. Perhaps it's part of my nature to want to organize and control. But I've begun to realize that trying to be logical and practical isn't always being sensitive or supportive. I'm learning I don't always have to even understand. I just have to listen and do my best to see things from Lynn's perspective."

That, gentlemen, is very valuable advice. Perhaps it's a masculine trait to want to give advice, be practical, and solve the problem. We're itchy to take action; we want to *do* something.

Yet there are times when the best course of action is simply to listen and try to see things from our wives' perspectives.

We Can Offer Relief

Sometimes, after we understand, give positive feedback, and listen, we can also do something that will help relieve motherhood stress. Once we know what job stresses present the biggest problem for our wives we can sometimes find creative ways to combat those particular stresses.

For example, getting up at night with kids was becoming a major stress on the wife of a friend of mine. She'd take a child to the bathroom or get someone a drink, then be wide awake for two hours before she could fall back to sleep. The result was constant exhaustion.

Once he understood the problem, my friend volunteered to take night duty. He can get up, care for a child's needs, and fall back to sleep the minute his head hits the pillow. His wife now feels rested and less stressed and he thinks a few minutes a night of lost sleep is a small price to pay for a happier, healthier wife.

One of the biggest stresses of motherhood is its *constant demands*. Some fathers who realize this have found creative ways to give their wives regular breaks. One dad we talked to takes charge every Saturday morning and sends his wife out by herself for breakfast. It's her time, time she can count on and look forward to every week when she can have peace and quiet to read and think. Another dad made it a priority to spend money on a babysitter/housekeeper one afternoon a week so his wife could have a break from the constant demands.

Some people we know do the "motherhood break" idea in even grander style. Once every three or four months, my friend Ron gives his wife a discount coupon for a one-night stay at some large, near-by hotel. He comes home on Friday afternoon to take over the house and the four kids. And his wife is on her own for the next thirty hours to read, sleep, browse through local malls, or do anything else she wants to do without having to worry about any of her regular motherhood responsibilities. She comes home so energized and rested and appreciative of his support that my friend considers the expense a very worthwhile investment in his wife and in their marriage.

Even if you don't feel your budget can afford a day's worth of meals and an overnight hotel stay for your wife, you could still try the mini-vacation idea. Just notify your wife she's off-duty and you'll take over all her responsibilities for a day, an afternoon, or even for a couple hours. Not only will the break from responsibility relieve some motherhood stress, but your affirmation of her needs will be a great stress reliever as well.

We Can Value Motherhood

Being a father isn't easy these days. We face a lot of stress, too. But after working on this book, I've come to the conclusion that motherhood stress is worse. And if you don't agree with me, just try doing a mother's job for a while.

I know I've never appreciated my wife more than I did a couple years ago when she taught part-time at a nearby college and I took care of four young children for one evening a week, all by myself. I'd prepare supper, feed the kids, and clear the table. Playing games and reading together would be fun. But by the time everyone was bathed, dressed in pajamas, and ready for bed, I'd be ready to crash. And when Debi walked in the door at 11:00 each Monday night, I always had an added appreciation for all the little things she did and the ease with which she did them.

It's at moments like those that I realize I don't appreciate enough the stresses of motherhood. As author Phyllis McGinley once wrote in an old book, *Sixpence in Her Shoe*, being a mother is "a difficult, a wrenching, sometimes an ungrateful job if it is looked on only as a job. Regarded as a profession, it is the noblest as it is the most ancient of the catalog. Let none persuade us differently or the world is lost indeed."

Perhaps the greatest thing we as husbands can do to combat motherhood stress is to look upon motherhood with that kind of perspective. Certainly it's a hard, stressful job. But it's also much more than a job. It's the noblest and most significant of professions.

If we'd just treat our wives as if we truly believed that, motherhood stress wouldn't be nearly as big a problem as it is.

Bibliography

Holly Atkinson, *Women and Fatigue* (New York: Pocket Books, 1985).

Ruth Schwartz Cowan, *More Work for Mother* (New York: Basic Books, Inc., 1983).

Louis Genevie and Eva Margolies, *The Motherhood Report* (New York: Macmillan, 1987).

Sheila Kitzinger, *Women as Mothers* (New York: Random House, 1978).

Robert S. Mendelsohn, *How to Raise a Healthy Child . . . In Spite of Your Doctor* (Chicago: Contemporary Books, Inc., 1984).

Donald Norfolk, *Executive Stress* (New York: Warner Books, 1986).

Charles Stroebel, *QR — The Quieting Reflex* (New York: Putnam, 1982).

Georgia Wiltkin-Lanoil, *The Female Stress Syndrome* (New York: Newmarket Press, 1984).

Susan Alexander Yates, *And Then I Had Kids* (Brentwood, Tennessee: Wolgemuth and Hyatt, 1988).

CALL FOR ENTRIES

Share Your Motherhood Wisdom

While working on this book, we heard so much good advice and so many stress-relief strategies that we're thinking about a book-length collection of motherhood stress relievers along the lines of the ideas shared in Chapter 15.

If you have some motherhood-stress-relief strategies you've used, stress-relieving advice you'd be willing to share with other mothers, stories about your motherhood stress and how you coped with it, or just some words of wisdom on reducing the stresses and discovering the joys of motherhood which you'd like to contribute to such a book—we'd like to hear from you.

Those contributions selected for publication will be credited in a source list which will include the names and hometowns of all contributors. (Please include your address and telephone number so we can contact you if we need additional information about your ideas.)

Send your motherhood wisdom to:

MOTHERHOOD STRESS RELIEF
Word Books
5221 North O'Connor, Suite 1000
Irving, TX 75039

People Making A Difference

Family Bookshelf offers the finest in good wholesome Christian literature, written by best-selling authors. All books are recommended by an Advisory Board of distinguished writers and editors.

We are also a vital part of a compassionate outreach called **Bowery Mission Ministries**. Our evangelical mission is devoted to helping the destitute of the inner city.

Our ministries date back more than a century and began by aiding homeless men lost in alcoholism. Now we also offer hope and Gospel strength to homeless, inner-city women and children. Our goal, in fact, is to end homelessness by teaching these deprived people how to be independent with the Lord by their side.

Downtrodden, homeless men are fed and clothed and may enter a discipleship program of one-on-one professional counseling, nutrition therapy and Bible study. This same Christian care is provided at our women and children's shelter.

We also welcome nearly 1,000 underprivileged children each summer at our Mont Lawn Camp located in Pennsylvania's beautiful Poconos. Here, impoverished youngsters enjoy the serenity of nature and an opportunity to receive the teachings of Jesus Christ. We also provide year-round assistance through teen activities, tutoring in reading and writing, Bible study, family counseling, college scholarships and vocational training.

During the spring, fall and winter months, our children's camp becomes a lovely retreat for religious gatherings of up to 200. Excellent accommodations include heated cabins, chapel, country-style meals and recreational facilities. Write to Paradise Lake Retreat Center, Box 252, Bushkill, PA 18324 or call: (717) 588-6067.

Still another vital part of our ministry is **Christian Herald magazine**. Our dynamic, bimonthly publication focuses on the true personal stories of men and women who, as "doers of the Word," are making a difference in their lives and the lives of others.

Bowery Mission Ministries are supported by voluntary contributions of individuals and bequests. Contributions are tax deductible. Checks should be made payable to Bowery Mission.

 **Fully accredited Member
of the Evangelical Council
for Financial Accountability**

Every Monday morning, our ministries staff joins together in prayer. If you have a prayer request for yourself or a loved one, simply write to us.

 Administrative Office:
40 Overlook Drive, Chappaqua,
New York 10514 Telephone: (914) 769-9000